●●●architecture in context

First published 1997 by
Könemann Verlagsgesellschaft mbH
Bonner Straße 126
D–50968 Köln

ISBN 3–89508–270–8 Könemann

© Könemann Verlagsgesellschaft
mbH 1997
Bonner Straße 126
D–50968 Köln

Published in the UK by
●●●ellipsis london limited
55 Charlotte Road
London EC2A 3QT

ISBN 1–899858–23–7 ellipsis

Designed and produced by
●●●ellipsis london limited

Photography by James Morris,
London
Text by Ingerid Helsing Almaas
Drawings by Micha Manz
Translated into German by
Andreas Klatt
Translated into French by
Armelle Tardiveau

Printed and bound in China

Vienna

●●●architecture in context

Ingerid Helsing Almaas

photographs by

James Morris

●●●ellipsis Könemann

So no special significance should be attached to the name of the city. Like all big cities, it consisted of irregularity, change, sliding forward, not keeping in step, collisions of things and affairs, and fathomless points of silence in between, of paved ways and wilderness, of one great rhythmic throb and the perpetual discord and dislocation of all opposing rhythms, and as a whole resembled a seething, bubbling fluid in a vessel consisting of all the solid material of buildings, laws, regulations, and historical traditions.

Robert Musil, The Man Without Qualities, Vienna 1930 (translated by Eithne Wilkins and Ernst Kaiser, Perigree Books, New York 1980)

Any city is unbearable.

Whatever the original noble motivations for the formation of a city might be, a contemporary city, in its confusing and unstoppable vigour, embodies all the things usually abhorrent to what gives our life cohesion, gives it form. Whatever truth you swear by, in a city the opposite will also be true. There, where people are closer to each other than anywhere else, paradoxically the ideas of unity, of majority, of generality are rendered painfully untenable. Nothing makes us long for certainty more than living in the city – bewildered among the contradictions of urban life, we need consistency, we need repetition, we need criminals to be caught and put in gaol. We rely on an illusion of universally acceptable truth, and only through a tremendous effort of various mechanisms of defence and denial can we tolerate the uncertainties, contradictions, ambiguities, affronts, inequalities: the squalor and the splendour of a city.

A city has to be cared for like a sick body: it has to be cleaned, fed, medicated, protected, encouraged and entertained. Its streets must be swept, its rubbish disposed of, its taxes collected, noises baffled, air monitored, effluent redirected; and its inhabitants, who swarm across and through it like maggots, causing nothing but harm and deterioration to themselves and each other, must be isolated, disarmed and diverted. But this body never gets better, it never heals. And if neglected even for a moment, its disgruntled retaliation will be to let loose all our most terrifying visions of chaos: having tamed nature, the untamed forces of the urban jungle, of human nature unleashed, fill us with the deepest dread. The rapid deterioration of the uncontrolled organism of the city is represented in some form or other in most popular visions of the future, from the technoid fantasies of early science fiction, in which the dominant classes hover in shining domes high above the seething mass of crime and disease, to the post-apocalyptic scroungers of Mad Max and the wretched rain-soaked street life of Blade Runner.

On the other hand, the city is irresistible. Its sheer density, the absurd juxtapositions imposed by the proximity of its many contradictory elements, provide the human mind with infinite stimulation, accelerating the usual staid pace of life to a fantastic dance, a whirl, a waltz. Who will you be?

1 Michael Maier's article 'The best place for the knife'. *Die Presse*, 5–7 January 1996.
2 'Spring-cleaning on the streets of Vienna'. From *Die Presse*'s daily 'Wien-Journal', 2 March 1996.
3 'Housing construction grows again by 10 per cent in 1994'. *Die Presse*, 23 August 1994.
4 'Thank you, Mr Mayor!' Vienna's weekly events paper celebrates the end of Helmut Zilk's ten years in office. *Falter* no. 37, 1994.

1 Article de Michael Maier «Le meilleur endroit pour un couteau». *Die Presse* du 5-7 janvier 1996.
2 «Le nettoyage de printemps des rues de Vienne». Le supplément quotidien «Wien-Journal» de *Die Presse* du 2 mars 1996.
3 «La construction de logements a augmenté de 10 pour cent en 1994». *Die Presse* du 23 août 1994.
4 «Merci, M. Le Maire!». L'hebdomadaire des spectacles et événements de Vienne célèbre la fin des 10 années de fonction d'Helmut Zilk. *Falter* no. 37, 1994.

1 Michael Maiers Artikel »Wo das Messer am besten sitzt«. *Die Presse*, 5.-7. Januar 1996.
2 »Der Frühjahrsputz auf Wiens Straßen«. Aus dem täglichen »Wien-Journal« der *Presse*, 2. März 1996.
3 »Wohnbauvolumen wächst auch 1994 um zehn Prozent«. *Die Presse*, 23. August 1994.
4 »Danke, Herr Bürgermeister!«, Das Wiener Wochenmagazin feiert das zehnjährige Amtsjubiläum von Helmut Zilk. *Falter*, 37/94.

1

Es soll also auf den Namen der Stadt kein besonderer Wert gelegt werden. Wie alle großen Städte bestand sie aus Unregelmäßigkeit, Wechsel, Vorgleiten, Nichtschritthalten, Zusammenstößen von Dingen und Angelegenheiten, bodenlosen Punkten der Stille dazwischen, aus Bahnen und Ungebahntem, aus einem großen rhythmischen Schlag und der ewigen Verstimmung und Verschiebung aller Rhythmen gegeneinander, und glich im ganzen einer kochenden Blase, die in einem Gefäß ruht, das aus dem dauerhaften Stoff von Häusern, Gesetzen, Verordnungen und geschichtlichen Überlieferungen besteht.

Robert Musil, Der Mann ohne Eigenschaften, Wien 1930

Jede Stadt ist unerträglich.

Gleich aus welchen edlen Beweggründen eine Stadt entstanden sein mag – mit ihrer verwirrenden, unaufhaltsamen Dynamik verkörpert eine Stadt heute all das, was den gestaltenden, bindenden Kräften unseres Lebens zuwider ist. Auf welche Wahrheit man auch schwören mag, in einer Stadt trifft auch das Gegenteil zu. Dort, wo die Menschen enger zusammenleben als irgendwo sonst, werden paradoxerweise die Konzepte der Einheit, Mehrheit oder Allgemeinheit schmerzhaft unhaltbar. Nichts läßt uns stärker nach Gewißheit streben als das Leben in der Stadt – verwirrt von den Widersprüchen des städtischen Lebens brauchen wir Beständigkeit, brauchen wir Wiederholung, brauchen wir die Dingfestmachung krimineller Elemente. Wir sind abhängig von der Illusion einer universell akzeptablen Wahrheit und können nur durch einen ungeheuren Aufwand verschiedener Verteidigungs- und Verneinungsmechanismen all die Ungewißheiten, Widersprüche, Doppeldeutigkeiten, Affronts und Ungleichheiten ertragen: das Elend und den Glanz einer Stadt.

Eine Stadt muß man pflegen wie einen kranken Körper: Sie muß gereinigt werden, genährt, ärztlich versorgt, beschützt, gefördert und unterhalten. Ihre Straßen müssen gekehrt, ihr Abfall beseitigt, ihre Steuern eingenommen, ihr Lärm gedämpft, ihre Luft überwacht, ihre Abwässer abgeleitet werden; und ihre Einwohner, die wie Maden durch sie schwärmen und nur Schaden und Verfall für sich selbst und alle anderen bewirken, müssen isoliert, entwaffnet und abgelenkt werden. Aber dieser Körper kann sich niemals erholen, kann niemals heilen. Und wird er auch nur einen Augenblick lang vernachlässigt, so besteht seine ärgerliche Vergeltung

Der Frühjahrsputz auf Wiens Straßen lief Freitag früh kurze Zeit auf Hochtouren. Doch am Vormittag stellte neuerlich einsetzender Schneefall die Bemühungen der fleißigen „Saubermänner" wieder in Frage. Wenn das Wetter in den nächsten Tagen halbwegs wieder mitspielt, dann wartet auf den Straßendienst Schwerarbeit. Schließlich sind heuer vom Winterdienst rund 100.000 Tonnen Splittmaterial auf den vereisten Straßen, Gassen und Gehwegen verstreut worden. Väterchen Frost hat der Stadt Wien schöne Kosten beschert. Bisher hat der Winterdienst bereits mehr als 400 Millionen Schilling gekostet. Es wird Zeit, daß die Sonne die Wiener bald entschädigt. Photo: Harald Hofmeister

2

Il ne faut donc donner au nom de la ville aucune signification spéciale. Comme toutes les grandes villes, elle était faite d'irrégularité et de changement, de choses et d'affaires glissant l'une devant l'autre, refusant de marcher au pas, s'entrechoquant; intervalles de silence, voies de passage et ample pulsation rythmique, éternelle dissonance, éternel déséquilibre des rythmes; en gros, une sorte de liquide en ébullition dans quelque récipient fait de la substance durable des maisons, des lois, des prescriptions et des traditions historiques.
Robert Musil, L'Homme sans qualités, Vienne 1930 (traduit par Philippe Jaccottet, Seuil, Paris 1995)

Toutes les villes sont insupportables.

Quelles que soient les nobles intentions qui ont permis sa planification, la ville d'aujourd'hui incarne, par son dynamisme confus et inépuisable, tout ce qui ailleurs est exécrable et qui donne ici un sens et une forme à notre vie. Quelle que soit la vérité que l'on revendique, en ville, le contraire sera vrai aussi. Ici, les gens sont plus proches les uns des autres et pourtant les notions de communauté, de sagesse et de biens communs sont douloureusement absentes. Vivre en ville nous rend encore plus avides de certitudes. Déroutés par les contradictions de la vie urbaine, nous recherchons la cohérence et la répétition et il nous faut l'assurance que les criminels seront arrêtés et emprisonnés. On repose sur l'illusion d'une vérité universelle. C'est seulement par divers mécanismes de défense et de dénégation, en faisant d'énormes efforts, que l'on parvient à supporter les incertitudes, les contradictions, les ambiguïtés, les affronts et les inégalités, en d'autres termes, la misère et la splendeur de la ville.

La ville, telle le corps d'un malade, doit être lavée, nourrie, soignée, protégée, soutenue et divertie. Il faut balayer les rues, ramasser les ordures, collecter les impôts et contrôler la nuisance du bruit et le niveau de pollution et aussi recycler les eaux usées. Quant à ses habitants qui, tels des asticots, grouillent à l'intérieur et ne font rien d'autre que de se nuire, entre eux et à eux-mêmes, ils sont très probablement isolés, désarmés et déroutés. Et ce corps ne va jamais mieux, il ne recouvre jamais la santé. Et s'il est négligé, ne serait-ce qu'un bref instant, il usera des pires représailles que notre imagination puisse concevoir : le chaos. La nature est peut-être apprivoisée, mais voilà que les forces sauvages de la jungle urbaine et des hommes déchaînés nous inspirent les pires angoisses. La dégradation rapide de la ville fait, sous diverses formes, partie de notre représentation du futur : des premières sciences-fictions où les classes dominantes vivaient dans des palais et régnaient sur une masse grouillante de criminels et de malades aux parasites de l'après-apocalypse dans Mad Max ou des misérables de Blade Runner qui vivent dans la rue, trempés jusqu'aux os.

Mais la ville reste irrésistible. Son incroyable densité, ses juxtapositions absurdes, régies par la proximité de ses nombreux éléments contradictoires, offrent une stimulation inépuisable qui accélère le rythme habituel et tranquille de la vie et qui la

darin, unsere ärgsten Chaosvisionen zu entfesseln: Nach der Zähmung der Natur füllt uns die ungezähmte Macht des städtischen Dschungels, der entfesselten menschlichen Natur, mit tiefstem Grauen. Der rapide Verfall des unkontrollierten Stadtkörpers ist in der einen oder anderen Form in die meisten populären Zukunftsvisionen eingezogen – von den Techno-Phantasien der frühen Science-fiction-Literatur, wo die herrschende Klasse in schimmernden Domen hoch über der brodelnden Masse von Verbrechen und Krankheit schwebt, bis zu den postapokalyptischen Plünderern in Filmen wie Mad Max und dem verzweifelten, regendurchnäßten Straßenleben in Blade Runner.

Andererseits ist die Stadt unwiderstehlich. Ihre enorme Dichte, die absurden Juxta-

Wohnbauvolumen wächst auch 1994 um zehn Prozent

Die größte Wohnbautätigkeit wird in Wien, Tirol, Kärnten und Vorarlberg registriert.

WIEN (apa). Das Institut für Marktforschung im Bauwesen erwartet für 1994 einen Anstieg des Wohnbauvolumens um 10,5 (1993: 9,5) Prozent, für das Gesamtbauvolumen ein Plus von vier (1993: 1,5) Prozent. Damit liegt das Wachstum des Wohnbaus um zweieinhalb mal höher als jenes der gesamten Bauwirtschaft.

Nach Bundesländern dürfte heuer das Wohnbauvolumen mit 20 Prozent Zuwachs erneut in Wien am stärksten zulegen, gefolgt von Tirol mit 13,5, Kärnten mit zwölf und Vorarlberg mit zehn Prozent. Für die Steiermark wird ein Wachstum von 9,5 Prozent, für Niederösterreich von 7,5, für das Burgenland sieben und für Salzburg von 6,5 Prozent erwartet. Schlußlicht dürfte Oberösterreich mit einem Wachstum von 3,5 Prozent sein. Wesentlichen Einfluß auf das gute Ergebnis der Wiener Bauwirtschaft im Jahr 1993 übte vor allem von der öffentlichen Hand stark forcierte Wohnbau aus: Das Volumen stieg um 17 Prozent auf 14,6 Mrd. S. In Wien dürften heuer rund 10.000 neue Wohnungen gefördert werden, in Niederösterreich liegt die Zahl der 1994 geförderten Wohnungen bei zirka 12.000. In Kärnten, wo der Schwerpunkt heuer beim Mehrfamilienwohnbau liegt, erreicht das Wohnbauwachstum deutlich unter jenem von 1993 (30 Prozent).

1995 soll der Wohnbau nach Einschätzung der Marktforscher nur 6,5 Prozent zulegen, das gesamte Bauvolumen um 4,5 Prozent. Dieses Sinken der Wohnbau-Zuwachsrate wird deshalb erwartet, weil in diesem Bereich bereits ein sehr hohes Niveau erreicht worden ist und aufgrund der budgetären Situation bei Bund und Ländern keine extrem hohen Steigerungsraten mehr möglich sind. Das etwas stärkere Plus beim Gesamtvolumen wird auf die Wiederbelebung des privaten Nichtwohnbaus aufgrund des EU-Beitritts zurückgeführt. Das Volumen der Sanierungen, das in den letzten Jahren kontinuierlich gestiegen ist, soll 1995 um etwa drei Prozent wachsen.

3

Danke, Herr Bürgermeister!

ZEHN JAHRE ZILK Letzten Samstag lud Helmut Zilk zu seinem 10jährigen Amtsjubiläum alle am 10. September 1984 erkorenen Jung-Wienerinnen und Wiener in den Wurstelprater.

4

Your choice of identities is limitless. In a city you can step from one to the other effortlessly and live a life without consequence. What will you do? The buildings of the city can be the backdrops, the containers for every imaginable event, from the subtlest experience to the most depraved excess. Every imaginable human activity takes place in the city, in a mixture of anonymity and public scrutiny which makes the risk of discovery yet another source of excitement.

A city is characterised as much by its habits as by its architecture. What you can do in a city depends to a large extent on what people have done there before you. From the simplest of traffic regulations to the most complex unwritten rules of social conduct, systems to control the threatening chaos of the city are continuously forming and reforming.

In terms of habits, Vienna is a rich city. A former capital of an empire which in 1867 included Hungary, Czechoslovakia, half of Romania and parts of Italy, Poland and Russia, its self-esteem is still considerable, and its self-image as a wealthy city at the centre of Europe is still alive, if somewhat tarnished by the turbulent events of the twentieth century. Certain objects and rituals still sustain this image of Vienna, the most prominent being the ones which are the most lucrative for the tourist industry: the Vienna Boys' Choir in the Imperial Chapel early on a Sunday morning; the annual Opera Ball; the daily public training sessions of the Spanish Riding School; the queue of <u>Fiaker</u>, horse-drawn carts, alongside the Stephansdom; coffee in one of the many famous cafés, where tradition is served on a plate alongside your <u>kleine Braune</u> at no extra charge. These reassuring images are still there for you to feed and to feed on, and sitting with a coffee in the sun in the Volksgarten, between the spires of the town hall and the imperial lawns, listening to the buzz of people, trams and traffic circling the historic city out there on the Ringstrasse, the illusion seems a most agreeable one.

1 'Exciting things are possible'. *Kurier*, 22 July 1994. An extensive public debate about Laurids & Manfred Ortner's competition-winning project for a new museum quarter in the centre of Vienna raged throughout the early 1990s.
2 Viennese officials crying crocodile tears over the death of the museum quarter project. Cartoon by Ironimus, aka architect Gustav Peichl. *Die Presse*, 13 October 1994.
3 Mayor Helmut Zilk's last question time: the museum-quarter project has become a laughing-stock. *Die Presse*, 'Wien-Journal', 15 October 1994.
4 'Inner-city bar'. The American Bar by Adolf Loos offered for sale. *Die Presse*, 15 October 1994.

1 «Ici, il se passe des choses passionnantes». *Kurier* du 22 juillet 1994. Un grand débat public sur le projet lauréat, remporté par Laurids & Manfred Ortner, du concours du nouveau quartier des musées dans le centre de Vienne a fait fureur au début des années 90.
2 Fonctionnaires viennois pleurant à chaudes larmes l'enterrement du projet du Museumsquartier. Dessin de Ironimus, aka architecte Gustav Peichl. *Die Presse* du 13 octobre 1994.
3 La dernière apparition publique du Maire Helmut Zilk : le projet du Museumsquartier est devenu une source de plaisanterie. Le supplément quotidien «Wien-Journal» de *Die Presse* du 15 octobre 1994.
4 «Bar de centre-ville». Le American Bar d'Adolf Loos sur le marché. *Die Presse* du 15 octobre 1994.

1 »Da sind spannende Sachen möglich«, *Kurier*, 22. Juli 1994. Um den preisgekrönten Entwurf von Laurids & Manfred Ortner für ein neues Museumsquartier in der Wiener Innenstadt entspann sich Anfang der neunziger Jahre eine lebhafte öffentliche Debatte.
2 Wiener Bürokraten vergießen Krokodilstränen am Grab des Projekts Museumsquartier. Karikatur von Ironimus (ein Pseudonym des Architekten Gustav Peichl). *Die Presse*, 13. Oktober 1994.
3 Bürgermeister Zilks letzte Fragestunde. Das Projekt Museumsquartier wird nur noch belächelt. *Die Presse*, »Wien-Journal«, 15. Oktober 1994.
4 »Innenstadt-Bar«. Die amerikanische Bar von Adolf Loos steht zum Verkauf. *Die Presse*, 15. Oktober 1994.

3

positionen, erzwungen durch das enge Nebeneinander ihrer vielen gegensätzlichen Elemente, all das bietet dem menschlichen Geist endlose Anregungen und beschleunigt das ansonsten gemessene Lebenstempo zu einem phantastischen Tanz, zum Wirbel, zum Walzer. Wer wollen Sie sein? Es bieten sich unzählige Identitäten an, denn in einer Stadt kann man mühelos von einer in die andere steigen und ein Leben ohne Konsequenzen führen. Was wollen Sie tun? Die Gebäude der Stadt können als Kulissen fungieren, als Rahmen für jedes nur denkbare Ereignis, vom subtilsten Erlebnis bis zur verworfensten Ausschreitung. Jede nur denkbare menschliche Tätigkeit geht in der Stadt vor sich, in einer Mischung von Anonymität und öffentlicher Einsichtnahme, so daß die Entdeckungsgefahr noch ein zusätzliches Reizelement bietet.

Eine Stadt wird durch ihre Gewohnheiten ebenso gekennzeichnet wie durch ihre Architektur. Was man in einer Stadt tun kann, hängt davon ab, was ihre Bewohner bereits vorher getan haben. Von den simpelsten Verkehrsregeln bis zum kompliziertesten, ungeschriebenen Sittenkodex – die Systeme zur Kontrolle des drohenden Chaos werden kontinuierlich geformt und umgeformt.

Was Gewohnheiten betrifft, ist Wien eine reiche Stadt. Die Selbstachtung der Hauptstadt eines vergangenen Kaiserreichs, das noch 1867 Ungarn, die Tschechoslowakei, halb Rumänien sowie Teile Italiens, Polens und Rußlands umfaßte, ist weiterhin hoch, Wien versteht sich nach wie vor als reiche Stadt im Zentrum Europas, wenn auch der Glanz durch die turbulenten Ereignisse des 20. Jahrhunderts etwas abgeblättert ist. Gewisse Objekte und Rituale halten dieses Image von Wien weiter aufrecht: die Wiener Sängerknaben in der Hofkapelle jeden Sonntagmorgen, der alljährliche Opernball, die öffentliche Trainingsarbeit der Lippizaner-hengste in der Spanischen Hofreitschule, die schlangestehenden Fiaker-Kutschen neben dem Stephansdom und, nicht zu vergessen, der Kaffee in einem der berühmten Kaffee-häuser, wo man zusammen mit einem kleinen Braunen auch gleich ein Stück Tradition serviert bekommt – im Preis inbegriffen. An solche beruhigenden Bilder kann man sich halten und davon nähren – und wenn man dann so mit seinem kleinen Braunen im

transforme en une danse, un tourbillon, une valse. Qui serez-vous ? Le choix est illimité. Dans une ville, on peut passer d'une identité à l'autre sans grand effort et mener une vie sans conséquence. Que ferez-vous ? Les bâtiments d'une ville peuvent être des toiles de fond, les récipients de multiples événements qui iront de l'expérience la plus raffinée aux plus grandes débauches. Toutes les activités humaines sont renfermées dans la ville, dans un contexte qui mêle anonymat et observation des autres, et où la chance de faire une découverte est une source d'excitation supplémentaire.

La ville est autant caractérisée par ses traditions que par son architecture. Ce que l'on peut faire dans une ville dépend de ce que les autres ont fait avant vous. Les moyens

de contrôle du chaos menaçant ne cessent de se faire et de se défaire, que ce soit pour une chose aussi simple que de régler la circulation ou bien plus complexe, de comprendre les lois non dictées du comportement social.

En ce qui concerne les traditions, Vienne est une ville très riche. Ancienne capitale d'un empire qui, jusqu'en 1867, comprenait la Hongrie, la Tchécoslovaquie, la moitié de la Roumanie et certaines régions de l'Italie, de la Pologne et de la Russie, sa fierté est considérable et son image d'elle-même en tant que ville riche au coeur de l'Europe existe toujours, bien que ternie par les événements agités du 20ème siècle.

Certains objets et rituels nourrissent encore cette image de Vienne et les plus

importants sont aussi les plus lucratifs pour l'industrie du tourisme : le Wiener Sängerknaben dans la Chapelle Impériale tôt le dimanche matin, les séances d'entraînement quotidiennes de l'École Équestre Espagnole, l'enfilade de fiacres le long du Stephansdom, le café dans les cafés où la tradition est servie sur un plateau avec une noisette, sans supplément ! Ces images rassurantes sont toujours là et c'est vous qui les alimentez et qui les nourrissez, installé au soleil avec votre noisette, dans un jardin public, entre les flèches de la mairie et les pelouses impériales, à écouter le brouhaha des gens, des trams et de la circulation qui font un cercle autour de la Ringstrasse dans le centre-ville historique. L'illusion est des plus agréables.

Volksgarten in der Sonne sitzt, zwischen dem Rathausturm und dem kaiserlichen Park, dem Stimmengewirr und der Straßenbahn lauscht, die draußen auf der Ringstraße rund um die historische Innenstadt fährt, dann ist das tatsächlich eine höchst angenehme Illusion.

Penthouse Seilergasse

Rüdiger Lainer

The historical centre of Vienna is unusually well defined, circumscribed by a wide ring road, the Ringstrasse, which replaced the fortifications surrounding the former imperial capital during the second half of the eighteenth century. The inner city, like a box brimful with luscious confectionery, contains all the things tourists flock to the city to consume, a selection of civic delicacies that is Vienna's chief source of revenue. Obviously such important monuments cannot be called into question by the addition of new and radically different architectural solutions. So the inner city is surrounded by a mass of building-conservation legislation as inviolable as the former city walls.

The people who, since the acknowledged blunders of the 1960s and 1970s, have been allowed to make significant marks on this lucrative historical assembly can be counted on one hand: a rooftop addition by Coop Himmelblau, hardly visible from the ground, and Hans Hollein's Haas House. All the more astonishing, then, that Rüdiger Lainer has been able to complete the uncompromised construction of a rooftop addition in glass and steel on top of an old building only a stone's throw from the Stephansdom, the medieval cathedral of St Stephan, the very hub of conservationist interest.

Rüdiger Lainer: 'The officer in charge of our case had a reputation for being particularly conservative, but this turned out to be chiefly because in his experience most things ended up as heavy-looking disasters because the architect hadn't been able to build the design promised by the drawings. After an hour and a half of conversation, we managed to convince him that we would be able to build what we had designed, with the necessary visual lightness, and we were given permission.'

The basic structural system of the vertical extension is three simple concrete decks on an orthogonal steel frame. But the positioning of internal partitions and built-in furniture is determined by the spatial development and functional requirements, resulting in the breaking up of the orthogonal space.

There are no visual boundaries to these rooftop rooms, no reassuring materiality; only the surrounding buildings lend walls to the space. There is nothing mediating between the basin tap or the door handle and the city: rooftops, spires, streets. The only things which offer some protection from this crazy transparency are the plain timber doors in the façade, which reverse the usual relationship of an opening to a wall.

Down on the street there are a number of accepted ways in which you protect yourself from the proximity of other people. Here on the roof, you are unprepared for the sudden openness. But once the first shock subsides, and you realise that your privacy is still intact

Le centre historique de la ville de Vienne est extraordinairement bien défini. Il est délimité par une grande ceinture qui a remplacé les fortifications autour de l'ancienne capitale impériale, élevées au cours de la deuxième moitié du 18ème siècle. Telle une boîte débordante de délicieuses confiseries, la ville intra-muros contient toutes ces choses dont les touristes raffolent et qu'ils consomment en masse. Ce choix de friandises municipales constitue la principale source de revenus pour Vienne. Bien entendu, il est hors de question de remettre en cause des monuments aussi importants en élevant des projets d'une architecture nouvelle et radicalement différente. Ainsi, le centre historique est protégé par une législation pour la sauvegarde du patrimoine qui est tout aussi inviolable que les anciennes fortifications de la ville.

Dès que l'on a pris conscience des erreurs faites dans les années 60 et 70, le nombre de gens autorisés à intervenir de façon radicale sur ce site historique et lucratif s'est compté sur les doigts d'une seule main : Coop Himmelblau avec son ajout sur un toit qui est à peine visible de la rue et Hans Hollein avec la Maison Haas. Il est tout aussi surprenant que Rüdiger Lainer ait pu réaliser sans faire de compromis la construction d'un ajout en verre et acier sur le toit d'un vieil immeuble à quelques pas de la Stephansdom, la cathédrale médiévale de Saint Stéphane

Das historische Stadtzentrum Wiens ist ungewöhnlich gut definiert – umgeben von einer breiten Umgehung, der Ringstraße, die in der zweiten Hälfte des 18. Jahrhunderts die Stadtmauern der ehemaligen kaiserlichen Metropole ersetzte. Die Innere Stadt, wie dieses alte Zentrum genannt wird, enthält wie eine Schachtel köstlicher Schokoladebonbons alle jene Dinge, die Touristen so gern konsumieren – städtebauliche Leckerbissen, aus denen die Wiener Fremdenverkehrsindustrie ihre Haupteinnahmen zieht. Selbstverständlich dürfen solch bedeutungsvolle Monumente nicht durch neue, radikal kontrastierende Bauprojekte in Frage gestellt werden; daher ist die Innere Stadt von Substanz-schonungsgesetzen umgeben, die ebenso unüberwindbar sind wie einst die Wiener Stadtmauern.

Die Architekten, die heute – nach den eingestandenen Fehlern der 60er und 70er Jahre – die Genehmigung erhalten haben, signifikante Beiträge zu diesem lukrativen historischen Areal zu leisten, können an den Fingern einer Hand aufgezählt werden. Da ist eine Dachgestaltung von Coop Himmelblau, von der Straße aus kaum sichtbar, und am Stephansplatz das umstrittene Haas-Haus von Hans Hollein. Um so erstaunlicher ist es daher, daß Rüdiger Lainer imstande war, seine Glas- und Stahlkonstruktion auf dem Dach eines alten Gebäudes kompromißlos fertig-zustellen – nur einen Steinwurf entfernt von der mittelalterlichen Kathedrale des Stephansdoms, die das absolute Zentrum des Wiener Denkmalschutzes ist.

Dazu Rüdiger Lainer: »Der für unseren Fall zuständige Beamte stand im Ruf, ganz besonders konservativ zu sein; allerdings stellte sich dann heraus, daß nach seiner Erfahrung viele Bauwerke zu schwerfälligen Fiaskos wurden, weil ihre Architekten nicht imstande waren, die Ver-sprechungen ihrer Entwürfe einzuhalten. Im Verlauf eines einhalbstündigen Gesprächs vermochten wir ihn davon zu überzeugen, daß wir genau das bauen würden, was wir entworfen hatten, mit der nötigen optischen Luftigkeit, und so erhielten wir die Genehmigung.«

Der Aufbau besteht im Prinzip aus drei einfachen Betonflächen in einem

thanks to the sheer physical distance from the nearest stranger, a smile spreads across your face: all manner of delightful civic mischief is possible in this extraordinary place where you are invisible to others but can yourself survey all. Lying naked in the Jacuzzi in the rear unit, you can open a hinged glass panel and see the Stephansdom. And when that very private sheet of glass is pushed aside, the medieval stone giant acquires a new meaning: in addition to being a house of worship and a tourist attraction, it is with you as you soak in the warm water, as real as the bubbles and water jets and the smell of your soap. In your bathtub, looking at the Stephansdom, you are invincible. That is how fantastic a city is.

qui est au coeur des intérêts défendus par les conservateurs.

Architecte Rüdiger Lainer raconte : «le fonctionnaire responsable de notre affaire avait la réputation d'être particulièrement conservateur. En fait, cette attitude s'expliquait par de mauvaises expériences faites par le passé. Des immeubles s'étaient révélés au final grossiers et catastrophiques pour la simple raison que l'architecte n'avait pas su réaliser ce qu'il avait promis sur plan. Après plus d'une heure de discussions, nous sommes parvenus à le convaincre de notre capacité à construire ce que nous avions conçu sur plan, avec toute la clarté visuelle nécessaire, et l'autorisation nous a été accordée.»

La structure de base de l'extension verticale est faite de trois platelages en béton sur une ossature orthogonale en acier. La disposition des cloisons intérieures et des meubles encastrés est déterminée par l'aménagement de l'espace et des exigences fonctionnelles, ce qui s'est traduit en un découpage de l'espace orthogonal. Les pièces de cet ajout sur le toit ne présentent aucune limitation visuelle, ni matérialité rassurante. Ce sont les immeubles avoisinants qui constituent les murs de l'espace. Il n'y a aucune transition entre le robinet de l'évier ou la poignée de porte et les toits, les flèches et les rues de la ville. La seule chose qui protège de cette incroyable transparence sont les portes en bois brut dans la façade

qui renversent la relation d'ouverture, que l'on trouve habituellement, avec un mur. Dans la rue, il existe des comportements pratiqués par chacun d'entre nous qui nous permettent de nous protéger de la proximité des autres. Sur le toit, vous n'êtes pas préparés à cette exposition soudaine. Mais une fois le premier choc surmonté, on se rend compte que notre intimité est préservée grâce à la distance physique qui nous sépare de notre voisin le plus proche. Puis on sourit : c'est la vie en communauté, sous ses formes les plus espiègles et les plus charmantes. Ici, personne ne vous voit et pourtant vous pouvez tout observer. Étendu nu dans le jacuzzi situé à l'arrière de l'espace, on peut voir la Stephansdom en ouvrant la

tabatière. Et lorsque l'on pousse cette tabatière très privée sur le côté, ce géant en pierre médiévale prend une nouvelle dimension : non seulement c'est un lieu de culte et une attraction touristique mais c'est aussi votre compagnon pendant que vous trempez dans l'eau chaude, aussi vrai que les bulles, les jets d'eau et le parfum de votre savon. De votre baignoire, le regard posé sur la Stephansdom, vous vous sentez invincible. Et c'est cela qui fait qu'une ville est fabuleuse.

Orthogonalstahlrahmen; aber die Anordnung der Innenwände und der Einbaumöbel wurde durch die räumliche Entwicklung und die funktionellen Erfordernisse bestimmt, was eine Auflösung des Orthogonalraums bewirkte.

Diese Penthouse-Räume haben keine visuellen Begrenzungen, keine beruhigende Körperlichkeit; nur die umliegenden Gebäude geben dem Raum seine Wände. Da vermittelt nichts zwischen den Wasserhähnen oder der Türklinke und der Stadt: Dächern, Türmen, Straßen. Das einzige, was etwas Schutz vor dieser irren Transparenz gewährt, sind die einfachen Holztüren in der Fassade, die dadurch ihre eigentliche Funktion umkehren.

Unten auf der Straße gibt es Konventionen, die es einem ermöglichen, Distanz zu seinen Mitmenschen zu wahren. Hier auf dem Dach ist man auf die plötzliche Offenheit nicht vorbereitet. Doch wenn man den ersten Schock überwunden hat und erkennt, daß man dank der reinen Entfernung zum nächsten Unbekannten immer noch seine Privatsphäre völlig bewahrt, beginnt man langsam zu lächeln: Der schönste städtische Unfug wird möglich in diesen außergewöhnlichen Räumen, wo man für andere unsichtbar ist, selbst aber alles überblicken kann. Liegt man zum Beispiel im hinteren Raum nackt im Jacuzzi, kann man ein Klappfenster öffnen und auf den Stephansdom hinausblicken; schiebt man diese höchst

diskrete Scheibe beiseite, nimmt dieser mittelalterliche Steingigant eine ganz neue Bedeutung an: Das ist nicht nur ein Gotteshaus und eine Touristenattraktion, sondern er gesellt sich zum warmen Bad hinzu, so lebensnah wie das sprudelnde, spritzende Wasser und der Geruch der Seife. Hier in Ihrer Badewanne, mit Blick auf den Stephansdom, sind Sie ganz einfach unbesiegbar. So phantastisch kann eine Stadt sein.

1,3 The evenly spaced veneered doors are positioned to allow for a future division of the penthouse into ten small living units. It is currently divided into five units and used as office space.

2 Seen from the Jacuzzi in the rearmost unit, the city's main cathedral is in your bathroom. The bathrooms throughout are separated from the other rooms only by simple glass partitions, allowing for an unconventionally open way of life.

1,3 Le positionnement des portes contreplaquées et espacées régulièrement permet de diviser l'espace en dix unités habitables. L'espace, actuellement divisé en cinq unités, est prévu pour des bureaux.

2 Du jacuzzi à l'arrière de l'unité, la cathédrale de la ville est dans votre salle de bains. Toutes les salles de bains de l'espace sont séparées des autres pièces par de simple cloisons de verre, une façon de vivre très ouverte et peu conventionnelle.

1,3 Die in gleichmäßigen Abständen angeordneten Furniertüren ermöglichen eine spätere Unterteilung des Penthouses in kleinere Wohneinheiten. Derzeit besteht es aus fünf Einheiten und wird als Büro genutzt.

2 Aus dem Jacuzzi in der hintersten Einheit hat man den Eindruck, als gehörte der Stephansdom mit zur Einrichtung. Generell werden die Badezimmer nur durch einfache Glasscheiben von den anderen Räumen abgesondert. Das Resultat: ein unkonventionell offenes Lebensgefühl.

1

2

3

1 The roof-tile pattern of the
  Stephansdom seen through the
  glazed opening in the solid side
  wall of the penthouse. The fixing
  details of the glass are hidden
  from view wherever possible.
2 View of the rooftops of the
  inner city.

1 Motif des tuiles de la toiture de la
  Stephansdom vu par tabatière du
  côté du mur solide de l'espace.
  Les fixations de la vitre sont
  dissimulées dans le verre de façon à
  libérer la vue autant que possible.
2 Vue des toits du centre-ville.

1 Durch eine verglaste Mauer-
  öffnung erscheint das Dachmuster
  des Stephansdoms im Penthouse.
  Die Scheibe ist fast unsichtbar in
  das Mauerwerk eingelassen.
2 Ausblick über die Dächer der
  Innenstadt.

1

2

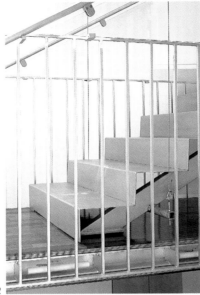

1, 4–5 Details of the main common stair connecting the two floors. The stair leads up to a walkway that crosses the entrance lobby to give access to the rear part of the penthouse.

2 The aluminium stair at the end of the walkway is hinged and swings up to reveal a cupboard or child's hiding place behind.

3 The walkway. The return on the right, which seems to turn straight into the wall, indicates where provision has been made for a possible future connection between currently separate units.

1, 4–5 Détails de l'escalier principal commun reliant les deux étages. L'escalier mène à un couloir qui croise le vestibule ouvrant sur la partie arrière de l'espace.

2 L'escalier en aluminium, à l'extrémité du passage, est articulé et se soulève pour révéler une cachette idéale pour un enfant ou un espace rangement.

3 Le passage. Le retour sur la droite, qui semble se terminer face au mur, indique les endroits où il est possible d'aménager des passages entre les unités actuellement en place.

1, 4–5 Detailansichten der gemeinsamen Haupttreppe zwischen den beiden Etagen. Die Treppe führt zu einem Gang hinauf, der die Eingangshalle überquert und den hinteren Teil des Penthouse zugänglich macht.

2 Die Aluminiumtreppe am Ende des Gangs ist scharniert und gibt beim Hochklappen einen Schrank oder ein Kinderversteck frei.

3 Der Gang. Was rechts direkt in die Wand zu führen scheint, ist de facto ein blinder Durchgang, der später einmal zwischen benachbarten Einheiten geöffnet werden könnte.

5

1 Bottom landing of the main
  common stair.
2 View from the main entrance
  through the lower right-hand unit.
3 Interior of the lower right-hand
  unit.
4 The main living space of the upper
  right-hand unit.

1 Palier de l'escalier principal
  commun, vu du bas.
2 Vue de l'entrée principale de
  l'unité droite du bas.
3 Intérieur de l'unité droite du bas.
4 L'espace principal de l'unité droite
  du haut.

1 Unterer Absatz der gemeinsamen
  Haupttreppe.
2 Blick vom Haupteingang durch
  die untere rechte Einheit.
3 Interieur der unteren rechten
  Einheit.
4 Der Hauptwohnraum der oberen
  rechten Einheit.

1

1

1,3–5 All the built-in furniture was
designed by the architect and
combines with the internal
partitioning systems to control
the tightly planned spaces and
to retain the intended flexibility.
Furniture and partitions are angled
in plan where necessary to allow
unrestricted movement through
the different spaces.
2 Bathroom of the rear unit with
Jacuzzi. A hinged glass panel opens
on to the corridor to allow a view
of the city.

1,3–5 Tous les meubles encastrés
sont conçus par l'architecte
et s'intègrent au système de
cloisonnement intérieur
permettant une conception à la
fois économique et flexible des
espaces. Le mobilier et les cloisons
sont par endroit taillés en biais
de manière à permettre une
circulation, la plus libre possible
dans les différents espaces.
2 La salle de bains et le jacuzzi de
l'unité arrière. La tabatière ouvrant
sur le couloir et offrant une vue
sur la ville.

1,3–5 Die vom Architekten entworfenen
Einbaumöbel dienen gemeinsam
mit den Raumteilern der Beherr-
schung der knapp konzipierten
Räume unter Wahrung der ein-
geplanten Flexibilität. Wo nötig,
sind Möbel und Raumteiler so
abgewinkelt, daß unbehinderte
Bewegung zwischen den verschiedenen Räumen möglich ist.
2 Badezimmer mit Jaccuzzi in der
hinteren Einheit. Eine scharnierte
Glasscheibe öffnet sich zum Korridor, um den Blick auf die Stadt
freizugeben.

2

3

4

5

Section A–A

10 metres

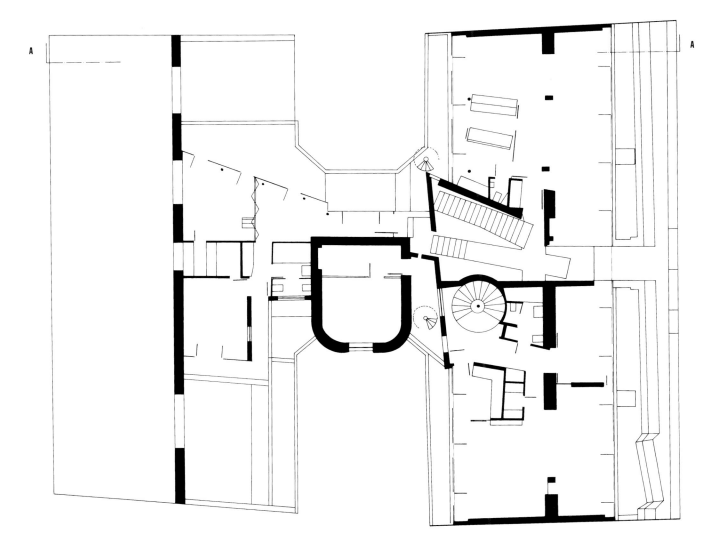

Plan: entrance level

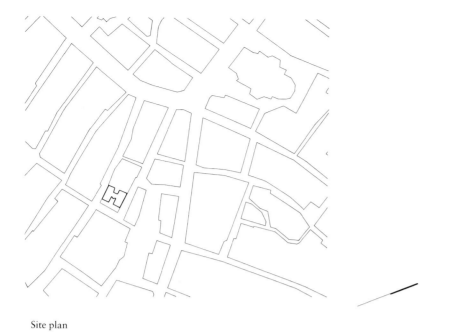

Site plan

Rüdiger Lainer
1995
Address Seilergasse 16, 1010 Vienna
Client Martin Schwanzer
Building owner Donau Versicherung
Project team Stephen Bidwell, Bernhard Moos,
Suki Sangha, Hannes Schild, Agnes
Stryjewska, Walter Boyer, Konrad
Rautter
Main contractor RELLA
Site agent Herbert Mühlegger
Environmental engineer Hans Dworak
Mechanical and electrical Introplan (Hannes Schwahofer)
Specialist steelwork Jordanits
Glass Hofmayr
Joinery Graschopf
Size 540 square metres
Construction cost AS 27,000/square metre
Prizes Excellence in Design Award,
American Institute of Architects,
London/UK Chapter

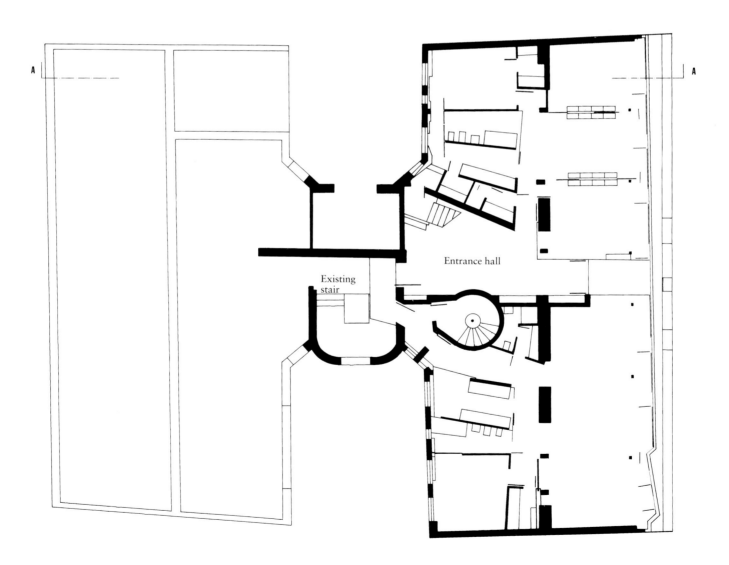

A — A

Existing stair

Entrance hall

Plan: top level

MAK-Café

Hermann Czech

Late one evening, after an argument with someone who swore that the MAK-Café was functionally useless and totally uninteresting architecturally, I asked the head waiter how the room functioned as a workplace. I expected the usual Viennese disapproval of all things new, but to my surprise the waiter told me he thought it was very good: there used to be, he said, a tradition in Vienna of large eating halls, similar to those you can still find in Paris, but nowadays the sweet little coffee-house has taken over as the symbol of all things Viennese and people have forgotten the large spaces – they don't quite know how to handle them. So customers enter the enormous, rectangular space of the MAK-Café with a certain respect, which makes a waiter's job a little easier. He also had no complaints about the functional provisions of the bar or kitchen areas. I felt vindicated.

The location of the MAK-Café is awkward: it was built inside an old room in the Museum of Applied Arts (MAK), raised up from the street with no separate entrance, as part of a general refurbishment of the museum in 1993. All the keys to the design lie in making good this lack of connection with the street, essential to the function of the café as a public place and not, in Hermann Czech's words, as a 'staff canteen'. As a result, all the elements of the new design point to their immediate surroundings or further into the city.

The new entrance from the Ringstrasse is made through the former side entrance to a rear court, where a massive wooden gate, built for carriages, opens to form an extension to the street and a few stone steps lead up to the new café door. The entrance stair cuts through the rustications at the base of the old building in seemingly total disregard for classical manners. Inside, the room itself, with its neo-renaissance painted ceiling and original tall windows on three sides, is left largely untouched apart from the addition of two freestanding bars/serveries at an angle in the middle, pointing east through the new exit towards the museum garden. The black glass tabletops reflect the ornate ceiling or the windows and branches of trees.

When asked the question, 'Who still represents a "Viennese tradition" in architecture?,' most architects I have spoken to in Vienna have mentioned Hermann Czech. It seems that Czech is not afraid to take hold of the picturesque aspects of the architecture of the past, which embody something usually beyond the reach of a more diagrammatic, less imaginative modernism. This he does not by use of the representational icons of post-modernism but by a combination of clarity of intention in the new functions and sensitive and inspired, even ironic, play with the existing elements. The result

Un soir tard, après avoir discuté avec quelqu'un qui affirmait que le Café MAK est un espace qui ne fonctionne pas et qui ne présente aucun intérêt architectural, j'ai demandé au chef de rang comment il vivait son espace de travail. Je m'attendais à la désapprobation habituelle des Viennois pour tout ce qui est nouveau. Mais, à ma grande surprise, il m'a dit qu'il le trouvait très bien. Autrefois, m'a-t-il expliqué, il y avait à Vienne une tradition de grandes brasseries, comme celles que l'on trouve encore à Paris. Aujourd'hui, ce sont les cafés petits et confortables qui sont devenus le symbole de Vienne et ses viennoiseries. Les gens ont oublié ces grands espaces et ne savent plus très bien comment les gérer. Au Café MAK, par

Spätabends – nach einer hitzigen Debatte mit jemandem, der Stein und Bein geschworen hatte, das MAK-Café sei funktionell unbrauchbar und architektonisch völlig uninteressant – fragte ich den Oberkellner, wie gut es sich in dem Raum arbeiten läßt. Ich erwartete die übliche Wiener Mißbilligung für alle neuen Dinge, doch zu meiner Überraschung hatte der Mann nur Gutes zu sagen: Es habe in Wien früher einmal eine Tradition für große Lokale gegeben, wie man sie heute noch in Paris findet, nun aber symbolisierten hübsche kleine Kaffeehäuser alles Wienerische, und die Menschen hätten die großen Räume vergessen – sie wüßten nicht, was sie damit anfangen sollten. Und so beträten die Gäste jetzt den riesigen, rechteckigen Raum des MAK-Cafés mit einem gewissen Respekt – das mache die Aufgabe des Kellners etwas leichter. Er hatte auch keinerlei Klagen über die funktionellen Eigenschaften von Bar oder Küche. Ich fühlte mich gerechtfertigt.

Etwas umständlich ist allerdings die Lage des MAK-Cafés; es wurde 1993 als Teil einer allgemeinen Renovierung in einem alten Raum des Museums für angewandte Kunst (MAK) eingerichtet, über der Straßenebene und ohne separaten Eingang. Alle Designelemente zielten darauf ab, diesen Mangel an direktem Kontakt mit der Straße gutzumachen – ungemein wichtig für die Funktion eines Kaffeehauses als öffentliches Lokal und nicht als Kantine, um mit Hermann Czech zu sprechen. Das Resultat ist, daß alle Elemente des neuen Designs auf die unmittelbare Umgebung oder weiter hinein in die Innenstadt hinweisen.

Der neue Eingang von der Ringstraße aus führt durch den früheren Seiteneingang zum Hinterhof des Museums, wo sich ein massives, seinerzeit für Kutschen gedachtes Holztor als eine Art Verlängerung zur Straße hin öffnet und einige Steinstufen hinauf zum neuen Kaffeehaustor führen. Die Eingangstreppe wurde durch die Rustika, die Bossenquadern an der Basis des alten Gebäudes, geführt, anscheinend ohne jede Rücksicht auf klassische Formen. Innen hingegen blieb der Raum selbst mit seinen Neo-

is not demonstrative, the architecture remains a background to the life it contains, but it is there, as if to step in when conversation dries up or if your thoughts should falter: a winter sky and the bare twigs of trees, reflected in black glass, beautiful beneath your dinner plate.

contre, les clients entrent dans l'immense espace rectangulaire avec un certain respect, ce qui facilite un peu le travail du serveur. Aucun reproche non plus à l'encontre des équipements fonctionnels du bar et des cuisines. Ces commentaires ont conforté mon opinion.

L'emplacement du Café MAK est malaisé. Construit en 1993, dans le cadre du programme de restauration du Musée pour les Arts Appliqués (MAK), il est situé dans une des salles du musée, au dessus du niveau de la rue et sans accès séparé. Toutes les clefs d'une conception réussie reposent sur le rééquilibrage de cette non-relation à la rue, si essentielle à la fonction d'un café en tant que lieu public, qui n'est pas une «cantine du personnel», comme

le dit Hermann Czech. En conséquence, tous les éléments de la conception attirent l'attention sur les environs ou sur la ville au delà.

Désormais, on a accès au café par la Ringstrasse en traversant l'ancienne entrée sur la cour intérieure où, une fois passé l'immense porte cochère en bois, on découvre un espace qui prolonge la rue et mène à la nouvelle entrée par quelques marches de pierre. L'escalier d'entrée traverse les bossages rustiques du rez-de-chaussée du vieux bâtiment sans aucune considération pour les styles classiques. Le café, avec son plafond peint dans un style néo-Renaissance et ses grandes fenêtres d'origine sur les trois côtés, n'a pratiquement pas été modifié. On a

seulement ajouté au milieu deux bars et offices libres en transversale qui pointent en direction de la nouvelle sortie du jardin du musée. Le verre fumé qui recouvre les tables reflète le plafond décoré ou les fenêtres et les branches des arbres. Quand on demande : «Qui représente encore la tradition viennoise dans le domaine de l'architecture ?», la plupart des architectes de Vienne citent Hermann Czech. Czech n'a pas peur, semble-t-il, de s'inspirer des aspects pittoresques de l'architecture du passé car ils ont souvent quelque chose qui fait défaut au modernisme, plus schématique et moins imaginatif. Il obtient ce résultat, non pas en utilisant les icônes figuratives du post-modernisme, mais en associant des nouvelles fonctions,

clairement affichées, à un jeu délicat, créatif et même ironique avec les éléments déjà existants. Le résultat n'est pas démonstratif. L'architecture demeure à l'arrière-plan de la vie qu'elle contient, tout en restant présente, prête à intervenir dès que la conversation tarit ou que votre esprit est soudain envahi par le doute. Et soudain un ciel d'hiver et des arbres aux branches nues se reflètent dans le verre noir de la table – que de beauté autour de votre couvert.

renaissance-Deckengemälden und den hohen Originalfenstern an drei Seiten weitgehend unverändert – abgesehen von zwei frei in der Mitte des Raums abgewinkelt zueinander stehenden Theken/Anrichten, nach Osten gerichtet durch den neuen Ausgang zum Museumsgarten. Die Tischflächen aus schwarzem Glas spiegeln die prunkvolle Decke wider, ebenso wie die Fenster und die Baumzweige draußen.

Auf die Frage: »Wer repräsentiert heute noch die ‚Wiener Tradition‘ in der Architektur?«, nannten mir die meisten Architekten in Wien den Namen Hermann Czech. Er, so scheint es, hat keine Scheu davor, sich der pittoresken Aspekte der alten Architektur zu bedienen, die etwas verkörpern, was den eher grafisch orien-

tierten, weniger einfallsreichen Modernismus häufig überfordert. Czech greift jedoch nicht auf Symbole der Postmoderne zurück, sondern kombiniert eine klare Zielsetzung für die neuen Funktionen mit einem sensiblen, inspirierten, ja sogar ironischen Spiel mit den vorhandenen Elementen. Das Ergebnis ist nicht aufdringlich – die Architektur bleibt stets Hintergrund zu dem Leben, das sie enthält, aber sie ist da, wie um einzugreifen, wenn sich eine Gesprächspause ergibt oder der Gedankenfluß stockt: ein Winterhimmel und die kahlen Baumzweige, die sich in Ihrer schwarzen Tischplatte widerspiegeln, wunderschön unter Ihrem Suppenteller.

1 Original window facing the
   Ringstrasse.
2,4 The entrance stair is lit by the last
   of the 'Johann Nestroy' lights
   originally designed to hang above
   the Reichsbrücke.
3,5 A round mirror facing the street
   reflects the Ringstrasse. A clear
   glass cut-out displays the menu
   of the day.
6 The new stone floor pattern is
   taken from a nineteenth-century
   pattern book by Leo von Klenze.
7–8 Views into the café through
   movable partitions.

1 Fenêtre d'origine donnant sur le
   Ringstrasse.
2,4 L'escalier d'entrée est éclairé par
   le dernier luminaire que Johann
   Nestroy a dessiné et conçu, à
   l'origine, pour le Reichsbrücke.
3,5 Un miroir rond donnant sur la
   rue où se réfléchit le Ringstrasse.
   On peut lire le menu du jour sur
   un vitrage transparent.
6 Le motif du sol, fait de pierres,
   est repris du motif d'un livre de
   Leo von Klenze.
7–8 Vues de l'intérieur du café des
   cloisons amovibles.

1 Originalfenster zur Ringstraße.
2,4 Die Eingangstreppe liegt unter dem
   Licht der letzten Johann-Nestroy-
   Lampen, die einmal für die Reichsbrücke vorgesehen waren.
3,5 In einem runden Spiegel verdoppelt
   sich die Ringstraße. Ein Klarglas-
   ausschnitt nimmt die Tageskarte
   auf.
6 Das Design des neuen Steinfuß-
   bodens ist einem Musterbuch Leo
   von Klenzes aus dem 19. Jahrhundert entnommen.
7–8 Blick in das Café durch bewegliche
   Raumteiler.

5

4 5

6

1–3, 6 Views of the interior. Fixed and moveable partitions divide the café, nearest the entrance, from the restaurant at the rear. The spun-aluminium light fittings show a relaxing disregard for whatever former ceremonies the room might have contained.
4 Industrial eyeball ventilation diffusers.
5 View into one of the rooms of the museum's permanent collection through an opening identical in size and proportion to the mirror by the entrance.

1–3, 6 Vues du café. Les cloisons fixes et amovibles divisent le café, situé près de l'entrée, du restaurant à l'arrière. Les lustres en aluminium centrifugé ignorent les coutumes dont cette pièce a autrefois été témoin.
4 Diffuseurs d'air industriels en forme de globe d'oeil.
5 Vue dans une des salles de la collection permanente du musée par une ouverture de taille et proportion égales au miroir de l'entrée.

1–3, 6 Das Café. Feste und bewegliche Raumteiler schirmen das Café am Eingang vom Restaurant weiter hinten ab. Die Alu-Leuchtkörper zeugen von beruhigender Respektlosigkeit vor der zeremoniellen Vergangenheit dieser Räume.
4 Industrielle Belüftungsdiffusoren.
5 Blick in einen der Räume für die Dauerausstellung des Museums, durch eine in Größe und Proportion mit dem Spiegel am Eingang indentische Öffnung.

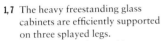

1,7 The heavy freestanding glass
cabinets are efficiently supported
on three splayed legs.
2,4 The chairs are designed by
Hermann Czech for furniture-
makers Thonet.
 3 Support brackets for the wall-
mounted aluminium light fittings.
Industrial details provide an
informal contrast to the original
room.
 5 The polished black glass tabletops
reflect the neo-renaissance
decorated ceiling.
 6 Leather-upholstered seats.

1,7 Les grandes vitrines tiennent sur
trois pieds orientés vers l'extérieur.
2,4 Chaises conçues par Hermann
Czech pour Thonet, un fabricant
de meubles.
 3 Supports des éclairages muraux
en aluminium. Le fini industriel
contraste avec le style traditionnel
de la salle.
 5 Le verre fumé poli, qui recouvre
les tables, reflète la décoration néo-
renaissance du plafond.
 6 Sièges en cuir.

1,7 Die schweren, freistehenden
Glasschränke ruhen sicher auf
drei gespreizten Füßen.
2,4 Die Stühle sind ein Entwurf
Hermann Czechs für den Möbel-
hersteller Thonet.
 3 Halterungen für die wandmont-
tierten Alu-Leuchtkörper. Industrielle Details sorgen für einen
ungezwungenen Kontrast mit
dem historischen Raum.
 5 Die polierten Tischplatten aus
schwarzem Glas reflektieren die
im Neorenaissancestil gehaltene
Decke.
 6 Ledersitze.

4

5

6

7

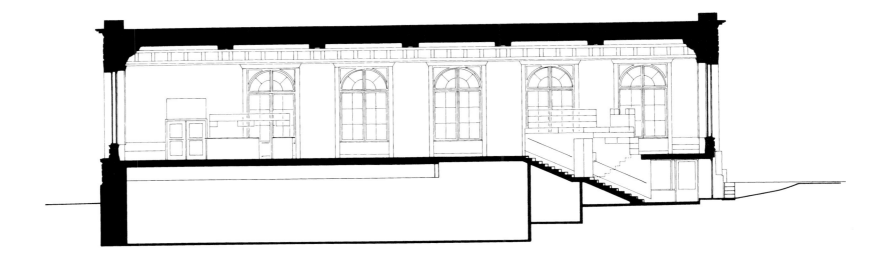

Section A–A

10 metres

Plan: basement level, staff facilities and kitchen

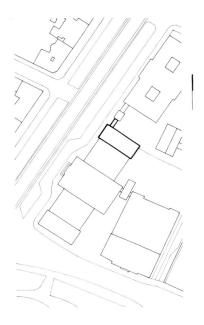

Site plan

Hermann Czech
1993
Address Stubenring 5, 1010 Vienna
Client Österreichisches Museum für
Angewandte Kunst (MAK)
Project team Margarita McGrath, Thomas Roth

Museum renovation project team
Architect Sepp Müller
Project management Immorent AG
Structural consultant Wolfdietrich Ziesel
Lighting consultant Rudolf Lamprecht
Mechanical and electrical Allplan

Subcontractors
Joinery Leopold Schramböck
Furniture Thonet Vienna
Chair design by Hermann Czech
Upholstery Manfred Glassl
Kitchen furnishing Fa. Lohberger
Size 500 square metres
Contract value AS 4.8 million excluding structural
work

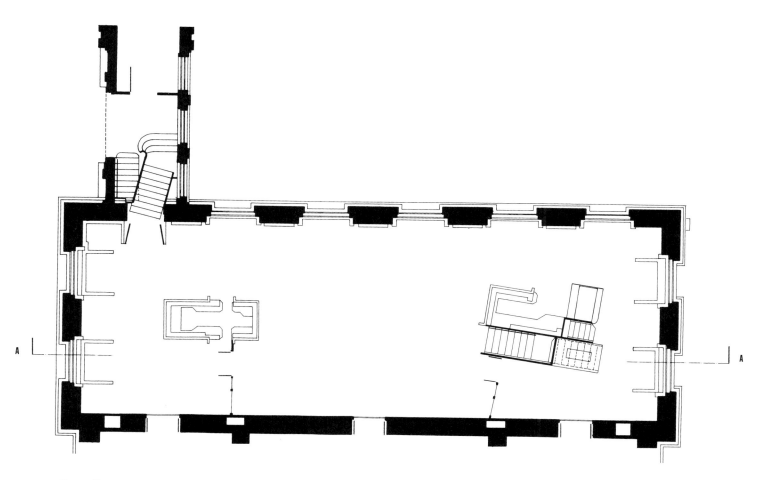

Plan: café

Moments of nostalgic blindness are brief exceptions within the constant effort to make sense, to understand, which faces the citizen of a metropolis. The strain of this effort affects people in different cities in different ways: it makes Londoners cynical and sarcastic, it makes Scandinavians sad and insecure and it makes the Viennese aggressive. These urban habits affect the work of the city's architects. The city bureaucracy, famously inflated since the loss of the empire; the strong, even crippling social hierarchy which controls the real or perceived positions of power in the city, be they cultural, academic, financial or political; the resulting intrigues, intolerance and small-mindedness – all this is part of the context in which architecture is produced and received.

When Michael Maier, editor-in-chief of one of the main independent national newspapers, Die Presse, left his post at the end of 1995 to transfer to the Berliner Zeitung, he felt compelled to summarise his years in Vienna in an article entitled 'The best place for the knife' (Die Presse supplement 'Spektrum', 5-7 January 1996). Over two pages he recounts his encounters with the Viennese; their officiousness and obsession with each other's titles; their two-facedness; their quick and fatal prejudices. He ends: 'I now know that charm can be a form of aggression. I now know that pleasantry can hide the most revolting brutality. I now know that politeness can be another form of rudeness.'

Maier also refers to the city's architecture, with a warning to the Viennese: 'Don't see yourselves too much in your beautiful old buildings.' For the physicality of Vienna still reinforces the city's imperial image and provides it with a sense of permanence as well as of achievement: the palaces of the Hofburg, now open to the citizens of the republic; the well-polished brass and stone of the luxurious shops along the Graben and Kärntnerstrasse; the sun-filled courtyards of the Red Vienna housing complexes of the 1920s and 1930s; the vineyards on the hills bordering the Vienna Forest; the flat fields to the south and east. Think of a city. What is it made from? The small things, the souvenirs: the public communions of the Sachertorte and the Würstl Stand, the disapproving elderly ladies with their small disapproving dogs, the marvellous public-transport system,

the Turkish immigrants at the Saturday flea market, the wet paper napkins under the glass of water accompanying your Melange, the smell of cheap soap that fills your hotel room in the morning, the colour of the river Wien late at night, running low.

As much as the Viennese take great pride in their monuments of the past, the present developments of the city also receive a great deal of public attention. The Viennese have strong civic sensibilities, they are highly critical, complain incessantly and expect a lot from their city and its authorities. Important new building projects are regularly scrutinised in the press. The local and national newspapers have special sections devoted to civic issues, such as Die Presse's 'Wien-Journal' and the weekly events paper

1–4 Viennese food, including Wiener Schnitzel in the form of the Stephansdom (4).

1–4 Plats viennois, dont un Wienerschnitzel à l'aspect de la Stephansdom (4).

1–4 Kulinarisches aus Wien, wie Schnitzel in Gestalt des Stephansdoms (4).

1

2

Mais ces moments de nostalgie aveugle sont des privilèges au milieu de l'effort que les habitants d'une métropole doivent en permanence fournir pour donner un sens à leur vie en ville. Cet effort affecte les habitants de toutes les villes, sous des formes diverses. Les Londoniens en deviennent cyniques et sarcastiques, les Scandinaves tristes et peu sûrs d'eux. Quant aux Viennois, ils en deviennent agressifs. Ces caractéristiques influencent le travail des architectes.

La bureaucratie de la municipalité, comme tout le monde le sait, s'est accrue depuis la chute de l'Empire. La hiérarchie sociale est très présente, voire écrasante, et régit les positions d'influence, réelles ou imaginées, sur le plan culturel, académique, financier ou

Momente nostalgischer Blindheit sind nur kurze Pausen in der andauernden Suche nach Sinn, nach Verständnis, die alle Bürger einer Metropole beschäftigt. Dieses mühevolle Be-streben beeinflußt die Einwohner verschie-dener Städte auf verschiedene Weise: Es macht die Londoner zynisch und sarkastisch und die Skandinavier traurig und unsicher – die Wiener aber macht es aggressiv. Diese städtischen Angewohnheiten beeinflussen auch die Baumeister Wiens. Die seit dem Verlust des Kaiserreiches bekanntlich aufge-blähte städtische Bürokratie, die starke, oft lähmende Gesellschaftshierarchie, die die wirklichen oder vermeintlichen kulturellen, akademischen, finanziellen und politischen Machtpositionen in der Stadt kontrolliert, und schließlich die daraus erwachsenden Intrigen,

die Intoleranz und die Engstirnigkeit – all das ist Teil des Kontexts, in dem Architektur erzeugt und aufgenommen wird. Als Michael Maier, Chefredakteur der wichtigsten über-regionalen österreichischen Tageszeitung Die Presse, Ende 1995 zur Berliner Zeitung überwechselte, fühlte er sich veranlaßt, seine drei Wiener Jahre in einem Artikel zusammen-zufassen, der den Titel trug: »Wo das Messer am besten sitzt« (Beilage »Spectrum«, 5.- 7. Januar 1996). Auf zwei Seiten schilderte er seine Begegnungen mit Wienern – ihren auf-dringlichen Diensteifer und ihre Besessenheit in Hinsicht auf Titel, ihre Falschheit und ihre schnell gefaßten, verheerenden Vorurteile. Maier schloß mit den Worten: »Ich weiß nun, daß Charme eine Angriffshaltung sein kann. Ich weiß nun, daß sich hinter der Gemütlich-

keit die abscheulichste Brutalität verbergen kann. Ich weiß nun, daß Höflichkeit eine andere Form von Ungezogenheit sein kann.«

Maier bezog sich auch auf die Architektur der Stadt, mit einer Warnung an die Wiener: »Bildet euch nicht allzuviel ein auf eure schönen historischen Gebäude.« Tatsache ist, daß die äußerliche Gestalt Wiens nach wie vor das kaiserliche Image der Stadt betont und ihr ein Gefühl der Dauer und Vollendung ver-leiht: die Paläste der Hofburg, heute den Bürgern der Republik geöffnet, die glitzern-den, gut polierten Messing- und Steinportale der Luxusläden am Graben, am Kohlmarkt und in der Kärntner Straße, die grünen, son-nigen Innenhöfe der sozialistischen Wohn-anlagen aus den zwanziger und dreißiger Jahren, die Weingärten auf den Hügeln des

Urban habits

3

politique. Les intrigues qui en résultent, l'intolérance et la petitesse d'esprit font partie du contexte dans lequel l'architecture est conçue et perçue. Lorsque Michael Maier quitta son poste de rédacteur en chef du journal national indépendant, Die Presse, pour aller au Berliner Zeitung, il écrivit un article intitulé «Le meilleur endroit pour un couteau» (Supplément «Spektrum» de Die Presse du 5-7 janvier 1996) qui résume ses trois années à Vienne. Sur deux pages, il raconte ses rencontres avec les Viennois, leur zèle et leur obsession pour les titres des uns et des autres, leur hypocrisie et leurs préjugés à l'emporte-pièce. Il termine en écrivant : «Je sais à présent que ce charme peut être une forme d'agression. Je sais aussi que la plaisanterie peut cacher une

brutalité des plus révoltantes. Je sais aujourd'hui que la politesse peut être une forme d'insolence.»

Maier parle aussi de l'architecture de la ville et met les Viennois en garde : «Ne pavoisez pas trop sur vos superbes anciennes bâtisses.» Car l'aspect physique de la ville met toujours en valeur l'image impériale de la ville et lui donne un sens de continuité et d'accomplissement, comme par exemple le palais des Hofburg, désormais ouvert aux citoyens de la république, les scintillantes boutiques de luxe, aux pierres et cuivres bien astiqués, sur le Graben et la Kärntnerstrasse, les cours intérieures inondées de soleil des cités de la Vienne rouge des années 20 et 30, les vignes sur les collines en bordure de la Forêt de Vienne, les champs plats au sud et à

l'est. Pensez à une ville. De quoi est-elle faite ? De détails, de souvenirs : les communions publiques des Sachertorte et des Würstl Stand, les vieilles dames désapprobatrices avec leurs chiens tout aussi désapprobateurs, le fantastique système de transport, les immigrants turcs sur le marché aux puces du samedi matin, les serviettes humides sous le verre d'eau qui accompagnent votre Melange (grand crème), l'odeur du savon bon marché qui envahit les chambres d'hôtel le matin, la couleur de l'eau de la Wien tard le soir qui coule tranquillement.

Les Viennois sont tout aussi fiers de leurs monuments historiques que des aménagements en cours auxquels ils portent le plus grand intérêt. Les Viennois ont un sens

civique très développé. Ils sont très critiques, se plaignent constamment et exigent beaucoup de leur ville et de ses autorités. La presse ne manque jamais de publier un article sur les nouveaux projets de construction. Les journaux locaux et nationaux ont des pages réservées aux sujets civiques, comme le «Wien-Journal» dans Die Presse et le «Stadtleben» dans le Falter, l'hebdomadaire des spectacles et événements, qui rend compte de tout, du déblayage de la neige aux meurtres commis en ville en passant par les derniers aménagements urbanistiques. Plutôt que d'être une affaire de spécialistes, l'architecture fait partie des conversations courantes et, bien que les voix conservatrices ne manquent pas de se

Wienerwalds und die flachen Felder südlich und östlich der Stadt. Stellen Sie sich doch eine Stadt vor. Woraus besteht sie? Aus den kleinen Dingen, die man mitnimmt wie ein Souvenir: die öffentlichen Treffen bei Sachertorte und am Würstelstand, die mißbilligend dreinschauenden älteren Damen mit ihren mißbilligend dreinschauenden Hündchen, die wundervollen öffentlichen Verkehrsmittel, die türkischen Gastarbeiter auf dem samstäglichen Naschmarkt, die feuchte Papierserviette unter dem Wasserglas, das stets Ihren Mokka begleitet, der Geruch billiger Seife in Ihrem billigen Hotelzimmer am Morgen, die Farbe des Wienflusses spätabends, wenn er ganz niedrig steht.

So stolz auch die Wiener auf die großen steinernen Zeugen ihrer Vergangenheit sind,

so schenken sie doch auch den gegenwärtigen baulichen Entwicklungen ihrer Stadt sehr viel Aufmerksamkeit. Die Wiener sind reaktionsfreudige Bürger, sie sind höchst kritisch, beschweren sich ununterbrochen und erwarten sehr viel von ihrer Stadt und deren Behörden. Wichtige neue Bauprojekte werden ständig in der Presse diskutiert; die lokalen und überregionalen Zeitungen widmen städtischen Angelegenheiten regelmäßige Spalten, wie etwa das »Wien-Journal« der Presse und das »Stadtleben« im Wiener Wochenmagazin Falter, wo über alles berichtet wird – von der Schneeräumung und lokalen Mordfällen bis zu jüngsten Entwicklungen in der Stadtplanung. Architektur ist hier nicht so sehr ein Anliegen von Fachleuten, sondern hat in diesen Diskussionen einen ganz natürlichen Platz, und

4

the Falter's 'Stadtleben', which report on everything from snow clearance and local murder cases to recent developments in city planning. Rather than being a specialist concern, architecture has a natural place within this discussion, and though the voices of conservation speak loudly, modern Vienna is also confident in its own abilities: the intentions of contemporary architecture, if not profoundly understood, are accepted, and new projects are appreciated as part of a general cultural achievement.

The public and media attention given to recent architecture has made the development of the city an area where political points can be scored. The planning policy for Vienna as presented in the 1994 development plan (STEP-94) reflected anticipated demographical changes which would see the city expand from 1.64 million in 1993 to 1.83 million in 2000. As a result of this anticipated population growth and the relative public and private wealth of the city, a massive expansion programme was instigated which aimed to provide 10,000 new housing units per year, surpassing even the much lauded inter-war efforts. This expansion was taking place mainly on greenfield sites in the outer districts, accompanied by the necessary new infrastructure, transport connections, schools, shops, churches, and so on. Chiefly thanks to the enlightened patronage of the councillor for city planning, Hannes Swoboda, who has a genuine interest in and understanding of architectural issues, this development also allowed for the production (if not the proliferation) of high-quality architectural design. Where possible, developers were forced to make use of the city's architectural talent for at least part of their production. And the local architects rose to the challenge. Extensive use of architectural competitions and informed commissioning have resulted in the construction of some truly remarkable buildings in recent years, particularly in social housing and school building. And the politicians involved have used these publicly funded enterprises to good effect to support the image of a city in growth.

In the last year or so, however, the population growth rate has declined and public funds are drying up: now politicians are trying to score points by reversing earlier policies. So 'city expansion' is being replaced by the cheaper option of 'revitalisation' of existing areas and the vast expansion to the south and north-east is being abandoned in favour of densification of the inner districts. The press speaks of 'Swoboda's Waterloo'. Local architects, however, remain cynical. They say the present focus on 'inner-city expansion' is advertised as a measure to avoid the infrastructure costs associated with the outer developments, but what the planners fail to take into account is that infrastructure will be needed in the inner districts too. The planning aims may change from one year to the next, but this is chiefly because the PR value in political terms is in the illusion of major changes. At the moment, it is cost reductions that grab the headlines.

1–2 Wiener Sängerknaben, the Vienna Boys' Choir.
3–4 Postcard views of Vienna.
  5 Record of the toilet-cleaning rota at the Hotel Sacher.

1–2 Le Wiener Sängerknaben, le choeur des garçons de Vienne.
3–4 Cartes postales de Vienne.
  5 Registre du tableau de service de nettoyage des toilettes de l'Hôtel Sacher.

1–2 Die Wiener Sängerknaben.
3–4 Wiener Ansichtskarten.
  5 Toilettendienstplan im Hotel Sacher.

1

2

faire entendre, la Vienne moderne a confiance en ses capacités. Même si elles ne sont pas intrinsèquement assimilées, les intentions de l'architecture contemporaine sont acceptées et les nouveaux projets compris comme faisant partie d'un accomplissement culturel général.

L'attention que portent le public et les médias à l'architecture récente a fait du développement de la ville un lieu où l'on marque des points politiques. La politique d'urbanisme de Vienne, comme elle est présentée dans le plan d'aménagement de 1994 (STEP–94) prend en compte les changements démographiques et prévoit une croissance de la population de 1,64 millions en 1993 à 1,83 millions en l'an 2000. Pour avoir anticipé cette augmentation du nombre

obwohl die Schützer des Stadtbildes lautstark auftreten, ist sich das moderne Wien seiner Fähigkeiten zuversichtlich bewußt: Die Intentionen moderner Architektur mögen nicht immer genau verstanden werden, sind aber doch meist akzeptabel, und neue Bauprojekte werden als Teil einer allgemeinen kulturellen Leistung gewürdigt.

Die Aufmerksamkeit der Öffentlichkeit und Medien im Hinblick auf neuere Bauprojekte hat die städtebauliche Entwicklung auch zu einer Arena für lohnende politische Auseinandersetzungen gemacht. Die Wiener Stadtentwicklungsplan 1994 (STEP-94) widmete sich demographischen Veränderungen, die eine Erhöhung der Einwohnerzahl von 1,64 Millionen im Jahre 1993 auf 1,83 Millionen im Jahre 2000 erwarten lassen. Ein Resultat dieses voraussichtlichen Bevölkerungswachstums sowie des relativen öffentlichen und privaten Wohlstands der Stadt war die Einleitung eines massiven Expansionsprogramms, das die Erstellung von 10 000 neuen Wohneinheiten pro Jahr vorsieht – mehr noch als bei den hochgerühmten Wohnbau-Aktivitäten Wiens in der Zeit zwischen den beiden Weltkriegen. Diese Expansion findet hauptsächlich auf Grüngelände in den Außenbezirken statt, begleitet von der erforderlichen neuen Infrastruktur: Transportverbindungen, Schulen, Geschäfte, Kirchen und so weiter. Vor allem der aufgeklärten Schirmherrschaft des Wiener Planungs-Stadtrats Hannes Swoboda, der echtes Interesse und Verständnis für architektonische Fragen gezeigt hat, ist es zu verdanken, daß diese Entwicklung zur Entstehung (aber nicht zu einer Überfülle) hochwertiger architektonischer Entwürfe geführt hat. Wo immer möglich wurden Bauunternehmer gezwungen, sich wenigstens für einen Teil ihres Projekts auf talentierte Wiener Architekten zu stützen. Diese zeigten sich der Herausforderung auch gewachsen. Zahlreiche Ausschreibungen und fundierte Entscheidungen haben in den letzten Jahren zur Errichtung wirklich bemerkenswerter Bauten geführt – besonders was Sozialwohnungen und Schulen betrifft. Auch die beteiligten Politiker haben diese öffentlich finanzierten Projekte optimal genutzt, um das Image einer wachsenden Großstadt zu fördern.

Seit etwa einem Jahr allerdings ist das Bevölkerungswachstum wieder rückläufig,

d'habitants ainsi que la valeur du patrimoine privé et public de la ville, un gigantesque programme d'expansion a été mis en place. Il comprend la construction de 10 000 nouveaux logements par an et dépasse de loin les louables efforts de l'entre-deux-guerres. Cette expansion se fait surtout ressentir en dehors de la ville où l'on aménage de nouvelles infrastructures, des liaisons de transport, des écoles, des magasins, des églises, etc. C'est surtout grâce au soutien éclairé de Hannes Swoboda, le conseiller municipal chargé de l'urbanisme, qui s'intéresse à l'architecture et en comprend les enjeux que ce programme a permis la production (si ce n'est la prolifération) de réalisations architecturales de qualité. Chaque fois que cela était possible, on a

exigé des promoteurs qu'ils fassent appel au talent des architectes viennois pour au moins une partie de la production. Et les architectes de la ville ont su relever le défi. La mise en place de nombreux concours d'architecture et commandes renseignées ont permis de voir s'édifier, au cours de ces dernières années, des oeuvres architecturales de grande qualité, notamment dans le domaine du logement social et de l'éducation. Les politiciens, impliqués dans ce projet, ont su faire un bon usage des entreprises financées par la municipalité pour renforcer l'image d'une ville en plein essor. Cependant, depuis environ un an, la population baisse et les fonds publics s'épuisent. Les hommes politiques, à présent, tentent de marquer des points en se retranchant dans leurs discours

antérieurs à cette période. Le développement de la ville cède le pas à la réhabilitation des quartiers existants tandis que le développement des quartiers du sud et du nord-est sont abandonnés au profit de la densification des arrondissements intra-muros. La presse parle du Waterloo de Swoboda. De leur côté, les architectes locaux n'en restent pas moins cyniques. Ils trouvent que l'intérêt dorénavant porté au «développement de la ville intra-muros» est promu comme une mesure permettant d'éviter les dépenses pour une infrastructure liée à l'aménagement de l'extérieur de la couronne. Mais les urbanistes ont oublié de prendre en compte le fait qu'une infrastructure sera aussi nécessaire pour les quartiers intra-muros. Les objectifs

d'aménagements changent d'une année à l'autre, mais en fait ce sont les efforts de relations publiques des politiques qui donnent l'illusion de changements radicaux... et de nos jours, ce sont les réductions des dépenses publiques qui font les grands titres.

und auch die öffentlichen Gelder sind knapp geworden; nun versuchen die Politiker, Punkte zu sammeln, indem sie frühere Initiativen rückgängig machen. An die Stelle der »Stadterweiterung« tritt die billigere Alternative einer »Stadterneuerung«, während die riesigen Expansionsflächen südlich und nordöstlich der Stadt zugunsten einer dichteren Besiedlung der Innenbezirke aufgegeben werden. Viele Neuerschließungsprojekte sind zu den Akten gelegt worden. Die Wiener Presse spricht nun von »Swobodas Waterloo«, während die lokalen Architekten zynisch bleiben; ihnen zufolge wird die gegenwärtige Konzentration auf »Innenstadterneuerung« zwar als Maßnahme zur Vermeidung der Infrastrukturkosten bei der Entwicklung der Wiener Randgebiete propagiert, aber die

Stadtplaner vergäßen dabei, daß auch für die innerstädtischen Entwicklungen eine neue Infrastruktur erforderlich sein werde. So mögen sich also die Planungsziele von einem Jahr aufs andere ändern, aber das liegt vor allem daran, daß die Illusion großer Umwälzungen große politische Werbewirksamkeit besitzt – und derzeit sind es eben Sparmaßnahmen, mit denen man Schlagzeilen machen kann.

SKALA-Bar

Driendl & Steixner

The SKALA bar and restaurant is unique both because of its construction and because of its commercially unattractive location. It is housed in the basement of a turn-of-the-century building in the densely built-up 7th district of Vienna, but it is not visible from the street – you have to know where to go: through an anonymous archway, across a private inner courtyard, down a flight of stairs and through an unmarked glass door. Inside, the long basement room is divided into a restaurant and a larger bar-café with an external yard, open only in summer, attached at the rear.

Georg Driendl: 'In 1987 the place was a rat-hole, an empty cellar. We have an office in the building above, and toyed with the idea of how nice it would be if there was a café or restaurant in the basement. Because of the inaccessibility of the location, it took a while before we found someone who was willing to back the idea, and even then it was intended only as a short-term venture. So within an existing volume, we wanted to make an interior which would be cleanable, which would not acquire patina, which would stay fresh to the end of its projected lifespan.

'To achieve this, we completely re-clad the cellar inside. The desire to keep it constantly fresh led to the idea of a clip-on interior, where any individual cladding element can be taken down and moved or replaced. There are no permanent surfaces. In 1987 this use of materials was very unusual and we received some heavy criticism – the traditional tendency in Vienna has been more towards disguising materials, treating them as a surface to be painted.'

Gerhard Steixner: 'Our choice of materials and the way in which we deployed them may have something to do with our involvement in film-making, where you go from one element to the next without a gradual transition. The different elements of the interior are treated differently: all the visible parts of the existing reinforced-concrete structure have been painted bright red. Visible existing brickwork has been cleaned and left exposed. The rest of the interior is made up of loose panels fixed with ball catches to a grid of simple steel frames bolted on to the old walls. The panels are made from plywood, glass, mirror, Perspex and cast fibreglass finished with silver spraypaint.'

The SKALA-Bar is a conjuring trick, as if a familiar object is suddenly covered by a shimmering silk handkerchief and your memories of it dissolve, unable to stick to the new, unexpected surfaces. On that new slate anything could be written, only to be washed away and rewritten the following night, permitting a temporary amnesia which is a relief in a city where the confusion of memories and reality is otherwise inescapable.

Die SKALA-Bar samt Restaurant ist einmalig – nicht nur in baulicher Hinsicht, sondern auch wegen ihrer kommerziell ungünstigen Lage. Sie befindet sich im Souterrain eines Gebäudes aus der Jahrhundertwende im stark verbauten 7. Wiener Gemeindebezirk und entzieht sich zudem dem Blick von der Straße – man muß einfach wissen, wo man hin will: durch einen unscheinbaren Torbogen, über einen privaten Innenhof, eine Treppe hinunter und durch eine anonyme Glastür. Der langgestreckte Kellerraum, in dem man sich nun befindet, unterteilt sich in ein Restaurant und ein größeres Bar-Café, das dahinter noch einen Außenhof hat.

Georg Driendl: »1987 war das bloß ein Rattenloch, ein leerer Keller. Wir haben oben im Haus ein Büro und oft mit der Idee gespielt, wie nett es wäre, im Souterrain ein Café oder ein Restaurant zu haben. Weil aber die Lage so ungünstig ist, dauerte es einige Zeit, bis wir einen willigen Geldgeber für dieses Projekt fanden – und selbst dann war nur an ein relativ kurzfristiges Unternehmen gedacht; innerhalb eines gegebenen Volumens wollten wir ein Interieur schaffen, das leicht zu reinigen war, keine Patina annehmen sollte und bis zum Ende seiner vorgesehenen Lebensdauer frisch und neu bleiben würde.

Um das zu erreichen, haben wir die Innenwände des Kellers komplett verkleidet. Das Bestreben, den Raum frisch zu erhalten, führte zu der Idee eines angeklippsten Interieurs, bei dem alle einzelnen Teile der Innenverkleidung abgenommen, ausgetauscht oder ersetzt werden können; es gibt keine permanenten Oberflächen. Eine solche Materialverwendung war 1987 noch sehr ungewöhnlich und stieß auf einige scharfe Kritik – traditionell neigte man in Wien mehr in Richtung auf die Verdeckung von Materialien durch Anstriche.«

Gerhard Steixner: »Unsere Auswahl von Materialien und die Art, wie wir sie eingesetzt haben, mag etwas mit unserer Filmarbeit zu tun haben, bei der man ohne schrittweise Übergänge von einem Element zum andern geht. Die verschiedenen Elemente des Interieurs wurden unterschiedlich behandelt: Alle sichtbaren Teile der schon bestehenden Stahlbetonstruktur

Le bar-restaurant SKALA est unique de par sa construction et son emplacement dans un quartier peu commerçant. Situé dans le sous-sol d'un bâtiment du début du siècle dans le 7ème arrondissement de Vienne qui est très construit, on ne l'aperçoit pas de la rue. Il faut connaître le chemin : on doit passer sous une immense arcade puis à travers une cours intérieure privée et descendre un escalier qui mène à une porte en verre sans marque. A l'intérieur, la longue salle est divisée en deux, d'un côté le restaurant et de l'autre le café-bar qui occupe une surface plus importante et qui est doté d'une cour extérieure attenante à l'arrière du bâtiment.

Georg Driendl raconte : «En 1987, l'endroit était un trou à rats, une cave vide.

Notre agence est au-dessus, dans les étages, et nous imaginions combien il serait agréable d'avoir un café ou un restaurant dans la cave. Parce que le lieu est difficile d'accès, il nous a fallu beaucoup de temps avant de trouver quelqu'un qui cautionne l'idée et, là encore, le projet devait rester provisoire. Dans un volume donné, nous voulions donc réaliser un intérieur facile à entretenir, qui resterait intact durant la durée du projet.

Pour y parvenir, nous avons entièrement revêtu l'intérieur de la cave. La volonté de le maintenir constamment propre nous a incité à utiliser un système de revêtement agrafé où chacun des éléments du revêtement pourrait être démonté,

déplacé ou remplacé. Aucune des surfaces n'est permanente. En 1987, cette utilisation des matériaux était peu répandue et nous avons été très critiqués pour cela. A Vienne la tendance est plutôt au déguisement des matériaux et au traitement des surfaces pour les peindre.»

Gerhard Steixner continue : «Notre choix des matériaux et la façon dont nous les avons utilisés ont peut-être été influencés par notre travail dans le cinéma où l'on passe d'un élément à l'autre sans transition progressive. Chaque élément de l'intérieur a été traité de façons différentes : on a peint en rouge vif toutes les parties visibles de l'ossature existante en béton armé. On a nettoyé la maçonnerie visible existante et on l'a

laissée à nu. Le reste de l'intérieur est fait de panneaux indépendants fixés à des loquets à billes sur un quadrillage en acier boulonné dans le mur. Les panneaux sont en contreplaqué, verre, miroir, Plexiglas et fibre de verre moulée et peint couleur argent à la bombe.»

Le SKALA est un tour de passe, une sorte d'objet familier soudain recouvert d'un mouchoir de soie chatoyante et dont on oublie aussitôt à quoi il ressemble, le souvenir ne s'attache pas aux nouvelles surfaces inattendues. Sur cette ardoise, tout s'écrit et s'efface pour être réécrit la nuit suivante. Il se produit ici une amnésie passagère bienvenue pour se soustraire la ville, cette ville où les souvenirs et la réalité se percutent sans cesse.

wurden hellrot gestrichen. Vorhandene Ziegelmauern wurden gereinigt und unverändert belassen. Der restliche Teil des Interieurs wurde mit losen Platten versehen, die mit Kugelschnäppern an einem einfachen Stahlgitterrahmen befestigt sind, der seinerseits mit den alten Wände verschraubt wurde. Die Platten bestehen aus Sperrholz, Glas, Spiegeln, Perspex und Glasfaserguß, überzogen mit Silberspritzlack.«

Das SKALA ist ein Zaubertrick – als ob ein vertrautes Objekt plötzlich von einem schimmernden Seidentuch überzogen wäre und die eigenen Erinnerungen daran verschwinden, ohne Haftvermögen an der neuen, unerwarteten Oberfläche. Auf diesen neuen »Tafeln« könnte alles mög-

liche geschrieben werden, nur um abgewischt und am nächsten Abend überschrieben zu werden; das ermöglicht einen zeitweisen Gedächtnisschwund – eine große Erleichterung in einer Stadt, wo man der Verschmelzung von Erinnerung und Realität sonst nicht entrinnen kann.

1–2 Doorgrips on the glass door of the entrance lobby.

3–4 Entrance lobby to toilets. All surfaces are smooth and cleanable, to allow no patina, to remain untouched by the passing of time.

5 Cloakroom.

6 Leather bench facing the rear courtyard. All wall surfaces are loose panels clipped on to the existing basement wall.

7 The rear of a panel showing the clip-on system. The plywood and fibreglass wall panels are held in place with ball catches and can be removed as required.

1–2 Poignées de porte vitrée du vestibule.

3–4 Vestibule des toilettes. Toutes les surfaces sont lisses et faciles d'entretien, conçues pour rester intactes à l'effet de patine et à l'usure du temps.

5 Équipement des vestiaires.

6 Banc en cuir face à la cour arrière. Toutes les surfaces des murs sont des panneaux indépendants fixés au mur existant de la cave.

7 Le dos d'un panneau montrant le système d'accrochage. Les panneaux muraux en contre-plaqué et fibre de verre sont tenus par des loquets à bille et peuvent être décrochés si besoin est.

1–2 Die Türgriffe an der Glastür der Eingangshalle.

3–4 Eingang zu den Toiletten. Alle Oberflächen sind glatt und pflege-leicht. Patina soll sich nicht bilden, um den Eindruck der Zeitlosigkeit zu wahren.

5 Garderobe.

6 Ledersitzbank mit Blick auf den Hinterhof. Die Kellerwände sind mit Wechselelementen verkleidet.

7 Auf der Rückseite eines Elements ist das Befestigungssystem sicht-bar. Die Sperrholz- und Glasfaser-paneele werden von Kugelschnäp-pern gehalten und können auf Wunsch abgenommen werden.

5

6

7

1–2 Seating details.
3–4 Restaurant.
5–6,8 General view of bar.
   7 Glass racks in the bar.
   9 Kinetic object by Christa
     Angelmeier. Two blackened
     glass sheets hold a mechanism
     emitting a constantly moving
     red laser beam.

1–2 Détails de chaise.
3–4 Restaurant.
5–6,8 Vue d'ensemble du bar.
   7 Casiers à verre du bar.
   9 Objet cinétique de Christa
     Angelmeier. Deux feuilles de verre
     foncées cachent un mécanisme qui
     émet en permanence un faisceau
     laser rouge en mouvement.

1–2 Sitzgruppe.
3–4 Restaurant.
5–6,8 Blick auf die Bar.
   7 Glasregal.
   9 Kinetisches Objekt von Christa
     Angelmeier. Zwei geschwärzte
     Glasscheiben halten einen Me-
     chanismus, der einen ständig be-
     wegten roten Laserstrahl abgibt.

7

8

9

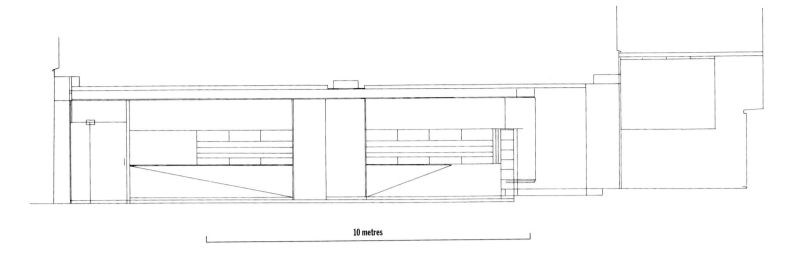

10 metres

Elevation of bar

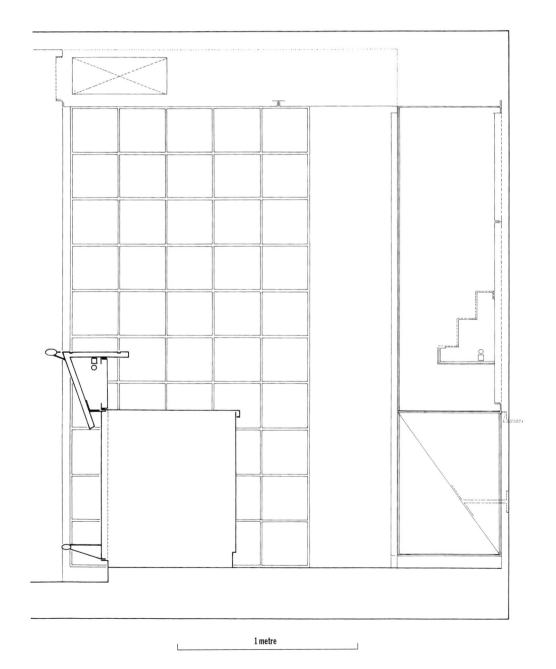

1 metre

Section through bar

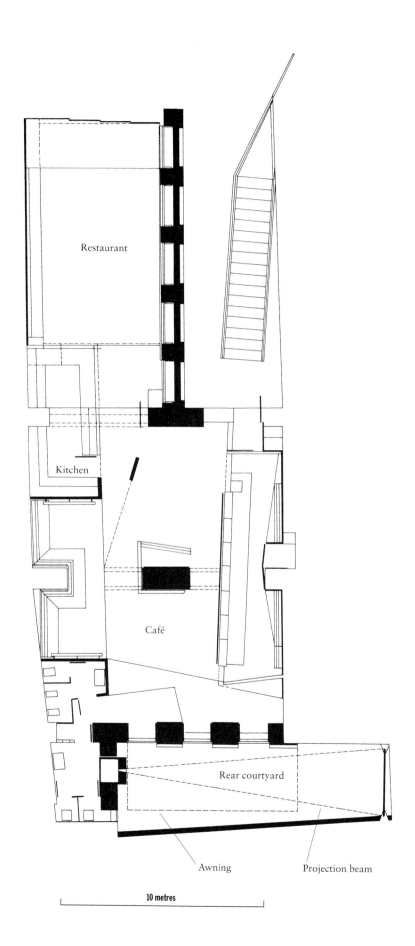

Restaurant

Kitchen

Café

Rear courtyard

Awning

Projection beam

|— 10 metres —|

Plan

Driendl & Steixner
1988
Address Neubaugasse 8, 1070 Vienna
Client Gastronomiebetrieb &
Kulturveranstaltungs GesmbH
Building owner DAW Leasing GesmbH, Vienna
Project team Georg Driendl and Gerhard
Steixner with Bruno Sandbichler
Services engineer Prof. Dipl. Ing. AMIRAS
Specialist steelwork Gerätewerk Matrei Reg. GesmbH,
Matrei
Glass ECKELT + CO, Steyr
Fibreglass panelling MALEX, Innsbruck
Stone Gerhard Weiss GesmbH, Vienna
Joinery Heinrich Karner, Frankenfels
Leather seating Leopold Patzak, Vienna
Kinetic object Christa Angelmeier
Bar/kitchen KREFFT Großküchentechnik,
Vienna
Size 250 square metres
Contract value AS 3 million

Kinkplatz School

Helmut Richter

In a building programme as ambitious as that for housing, Vienna is injecting AS 7 billion into more than 30 new schools. The Schulbauprogramm 2000 has become a regular showcase for contemporary architecture, and most of the good architects in Vienna have received a commission. For many, such as Driendl & Steixner or ARTEK, it has been the first opportunity to design a large public building for the capital.

Helmut Richter's school in the 14th district puts much contemporary Viennese architecture into perspective. With its glass roofs and steel structure, it is above all a terrific technical achievement. There is no tradition of steel-frame or glass construction in Vienna, no tradition of prefabrication – most of what is being built, and certainly most of the new public housing, is limited to cheap concrete frames and rendered blockwork with the occasional steel detail. The methods and materials used in Richter's school are simple and repeatable; it gains its power from a visible consistency, each decision a consequence of the last with no compromises along the way. And it cost no more than traditional massive construction methods: by working with the engineer on removing half the concrete and replacing it with a more carefully considered system of steel bracing, Richter was able to release money into other areas.

Located on a steeply sloping triangular site between a churchyard and a football field, the school has a straightforward plan – questioning pedagogical conventions is not part of the Schulbauprogramm brief. Three long blocks face the existing buildings to the north, with classrooms off slightly conical corridors connected by perpendicular galleries at the south end. The three levels of the gallery look out to the hills south of the city through enormous sloping sheets of glass which cover the triple-height gymnasium and the indoor vestibule.

Throughout the building you come right up against the details of the structure, you can see and feel how it is put together and how it works. What more could you ask of an educational building? The structure is left bare internally and all the services are visible. The corridor walls are yellow, the overhead cable trays blue, the lift shaft red. The rest of the building is the greys and silvers of concrete, steel and aluminium, and everywhere the green shimmer of the double glass.

The Viennese reaction to this magnificent building is peculiar. It ought to be the undisputed summit of the 'architectonic research into the future' that according to councillor for city planning Hannes Swoboda is the aim of the school-building programme. But in the public reaction there is the sense that Richter has crossed an invisible line: this building is simply too much. Even among architects, you come across sentiments like, 'Why did

1 Classroom.

1 Salle de classes.

1 Klassenzimmer.

La ville de Vienne a investi 7 milliards de Schilling Autrichiens dans un programme de construction de quelque 30 écoles, tout aussi ambitieux que celui du logement. Le Schulbauprogramm 2000 (programme de construction d'écoles pour l'an 2000) est devenu une vitrine de l'architecture contemporaine et la plupart des grands architectes de Vienne ont été invités à y participer. Pour nombre d'entre eux, comme par exemple Driendl & Steixner ou ARTEK, cette opération leur a offert la possibilité, pour la première fois, de concevoir un bâtiment public pour la ville. L'école de Helmut Richter qui est située dans le 14ème arrondissement met en perspective toute l'architecture viennoise. Avec ses toits de verre et son ossature en acier, c'est avant tout un grand exploit technique. Vienne n'a aucune tradition de constructions en verre ou préfabriquées ou d'ossatures en acier. La plupart des constructions, et bien entendu la plupart des nouveaux logements publics, se limitent à des ossatures en béton bon marché et à une maçonnerie en briques creuses enduites avec, par endroit, des détails en acier. Les méthodes et matériaux que Richter a utilisés pour son école sont simples et peuvent être reproduits. Son impact réside dans la cohérence évidente avec laquelle chaque décision a été prise, en fonction de la précédente, sans compromis. Par ailleurs, cette école n'a pas coûté plus cher qu'un bâtiment construit avec des méthodes traditionnelles et

Im Rahmen eines Bauprogramms, das nicht weniger ehrgeizig ist als das im Wohnungssektor, investiert Wien sieben Milliarden Schilling in die Errichtung von über 30 neuen Schulen. Das Schulbauprogramm 2000 ist zu einem regelrechten Schaufenster für zeitgenössische Architektur geworden, und die meisten guten Architekten Wiens haben Aufträge erhalten; vielen Baukanzleien, wie etwa Driendl & Steixner oder ARTEK, bot sich damit die erste Gelegenheit, ein großes öffentliches Gebäude in Wien errichten zu können.

Helmut Richters Schule im 14. Bezirk läßt viel von der zeitgenössischen Wiener Architektur in einem neuen Licht erscheinen. Mit ihren Glasdächern und ihrer Stahlstruktur ist diese Schule in erster Linie eine unerhörte technische Leistung. In Wien gibt es keine Bautradition von Stahlskelett- oder Glaskonstruktionen, keine Fertigbautradition – die meisten Bauwerke hier, besonders die meisten öffentlichen Bauten, bestehen aus den billigsten Betonrahmen und verputzten Blocksteinmauern mit gelegentlichen Stahleinlagen. Die in Richters Schule verwendeten Methoden und Materialien sind einfach und wiederholbar; das Gebäude bezieht seine Stärke aus einer sichtbaren Konsistenz – eine Entscheidung schließt sich folgerichtig und kompromißlos an die andere an. Die Kosten waren nicht höher als beim traditionellen Massenbetonbau; indem er zusammen mit dem Bauingenieur das Betonvolumen halbierte und durch ein klüger ausgedachtes System von Stahlversteifungen ersetzte, war Richter imstande, Geld für andere Aspekte freizusetzen.

Die Schule liegt auf einem stark abfallenden, dreieckigen Grundstück zwischen einer Kirche und einem Fußballplatz und verfolgt ein unkompliziertes Konzept – pädagogische Konventionen in Frage zu stellen ist nicht Sache des Wiener Schulbauprogramms. Drei lange Blöcke stehen den vorhandenen Gebäuden im Norden gegenüber, wobei die Klassenzimmer an leicht konischen Gängen durch rechtwinkelige Galerien am südlichen Ende verbunden werden. Die drei Ebenen dieser Galerien haben Ausblick auf die Hügellandschaft südlich der Stadt durch riesige,

he have to go and do that? Now he has ruined it for everybody, we'll never be allowed to experiment again,' rather than support for a colleague whose achievement should be the pride of the profession. Perhaps it is because Richter's building is so unviennese – it unashamedly exposes everything and refuses to play the usual titillating Viennese games of promise and deceit, and, worst of all, it is not embarrassed: like Frankenstein's monster, Richter's school bears witness to the facts of its construction and offers no option but acceptance on its own terms.

1

lourdes. Grâce à sa collaboration avec un ingénieur qui a déblayé la moitié du béton pour le remplacer par un système de contreventement en acier plus intelligemment conçu, Richter a pu redistribuer ailleurs l'économie ainsi faite.

Située sur un site triangulaire en pente aiguë, entre un cimetière près d'une église et un terrain de football, le plan de l'école est très simple. Remettre en cause les conventions pédagogiques ne fait pas partie du cahier des charges du Schulbauprogramm. Trois longs bâtiments se tiennent face aux bâtiments existants situés au nord avec des salles de classe excentrées des couloirs légèrement coniques qui sont reliées à des galeries perpendiculaires situées à l'extrémité sud.

Les trois niveaux de la galerie donnent sur les collines sud de la ville qu'on peut voir à travers les immenses panneaux de verre en pente et qui couvrent le gymnase et le hall d'entrée sur une hauteur de trois étages. Dans tous les espaces du bâtiment, on peut admirer les détails de la structure et l'on peut voir et comprendre la manière dont elle est conçue et dont elle fonctionne.

Que peut-on demander de plus à un bâtiment scolaire ? A l'intérieur, la structure et les équipements sont visibles à l'oeil nu. Les murs des couloirs sont jaunes, les goulottes en hauteur sont bleues, la cage d'ascenseur est rouge. Le reste du bâtiment est en béton peint gris ou argent, en acier et aluminium et partout un miroitement vert grâce au double

vitrage. La réaction des Viennois à propos de ce bâtiment magnifique est étrange. Il aurait dû être accueilli comme un très bel exemple de «recherche architectonique pour l'avenir», ce qui est l'objectif du programme, explique Hannes Swoboda, le conseiller municipal chargé de l'urbanisme. Mais, pour le public, Richter a franchi une limite invisible : ce bâtiment dépasse les bornes. Plutôt que de soutenir un confrère dont l'exploit fait honneur à la profession, les architectes expriment eux aussi des réserves : «Qu'avait-il besoin de faire une chose pareille ? Il a coupé l'herbe sous les pieds de tout le monde, on ne nous laissera plus rien faire de neuf.» Peut-être est-ce dû au fait que le bâtiment de Richter est contraire à la tradition viennoise.

Il expose, sans scrupule, tous ses aspects et se refuse à toute tentation, aussi titillante soit-elle, de mêler promesse et déception, si typique des réalisations viennoises. Et, pire encore, il le fait sans vergogne. A l'instar du monstre de Frankenstein, l'école de Richter expose les éléments de sa construction et n'offre aucune autre alternative que celle de l'accepter.

abgeschrägte Glasscheiben, die den Innenvorhof und die drei Stockwerke hohe Turnhalle überdecken.

Im ganzen Gebäude kann man direkt die Einzelheiten der Struktur erkennen. Man kann sehen und greifen, wie sie zusammengefügt wurde und wie sie funktioniert. Was kann man von einem Unterrichtsgebäude mehr verlangen? Die Innenstruktur wurde unbedeckt belassen, alle Installationen sind klar sichtbar. Die Korridorwände sind in Gelb, die darüber verlaufenden Kabelschächte in Blau, die Liftschächte in Rot gehalten; der Rest des Gebäudes zeigt die Grau- und Silbertöne von Beton, Stahl und Aluminium, und über dem Ganzen liegt der grüne Schimmer der Doppelverglasung.

Auf dieses großartige Gebäude hat Wien seltsam reagiert. Es sollte eigentlich der unbestrittene Höhepunkt jener »architektonischen Zukunftsforschung« sein, die laut Planungs-Stadtrat Hannes Swoboda das Ziel des Schulbauprogramms ist. Die Reaktion der Öffentlichkeit drückt jedoch das Empfinden aus, daß Helmut Richter hier eine unsichtbare Grenze überschritten hat: Dieses Gebäude ist einfach ... zuviel. Selbst von Architekten kann man Äußerungen hören wie: »Warum hat er das nur getan? Damit hat er es für alle verdorben – jetzt werden wir nie mehr experimentieren dürfen«, anstatt einen Kollegen zu unterstützen, dessen Leistung der Stolz seines Berufsstandes sein sollte. Vielleicht ist Richters Schule zu »unwienerisch«; sie

deckt alles schamlos auf und weigert sich, die aufreizenden Wiener Spielchen von Versprechen und Täuschung mitzuspielen, und, schlimmer noch, dieses Gebäude ist nicht verlegen, es entschuldigt sich nicht: Wie Frankensteins Monster legt auch Richters Schule ein klares Zeugnis ab von den Einzelheiten ihrer Konstruktion und läßt keine andere Wahl, als sie zu ihren eigenen Bedingungen zu akzeptieren.

1–3 Fire escapes at the end of a
classroom block.
4 General view from the entrance
side. The largest of the glass
roofs, covering the triple-height
gymnasium, has a free span of
25 metres.
5 View from the east. The little stalls
along the pavement sell flowers
and grave ornaments to visitors to
the churchyard across the street.

1–3 Escalier de secours à l'extrémité
du bloc des salles de classes.
4 Vue d'ensemble, côté entrée.
Le plus grand des toits en verre
qui abrite le gymnase, d'une triple
hauteur, est d'une portée de 25
mètres.
5 Vue côté est. Étalages de
marchands le long du trottoir
où l'on peut acheter des fleurs et
des ornements pour les pierres
tombales du cimetière situé de
l'autre côté de la rue.

1–3 Feuertreppe am Ende des Unterrichtsblocks.
4 Ansicht der Eingangsseite. Das
größte Glasdach, das die drei
Stockwerke hohe Turnhalle überdeckt, hat eine freie Spannweite
von 25 m.
5 Ostansicht. Die kleinen Stände
am Gehsteig verkaufen Blumen
und Grabschmuck an Besucher
des Friedhofs auf der anderen
Straßenseite.

4

5

1 Entrance ramp.
2 The lift shaft is covered with red rubberised sheeting.
3 School garden between two of the classroom blocks. External cross-bracing avoids the need for a mass concrete construction, the usual choice for public buildings in Vienna.
4 A transverse four-storey gallery connects the three classroom blocks horizontally and vertically and looks out into the glazed gymnasium and assembly hall, allowing the children to get up close to the details of the construction.

1 Rampe d'entrée.
2 La cage d'ascenseur est enveloppée d'un film en caoutchouc rouge.
3 Jardin de l'école entre deux blocs de salles de classes. Les croisillons extérieurs permettent d'éviter une construction massive en béton typique des bâtiments publics viennois.
4 Une galerie transversale de quatre étages relie horizontalement et verticalement les trois blocs de salle de classes et donne sur le gymnase vitré et le hall de réunion, permettant aux écoliers de voir de près les détails de construction.

1 Eingangsrampe.
2 Der Liftschacht ist mit rotem Gummibelag bedeckt.
3 Der Schulgarten zwischen zwei Unterrichtsblöcken. Der äußere Kreuzverband ermöglicht den Verzicht auf die im öffentlichen Bauwesen Wiens allzu vertraute Massenbetonkonstruktion.
4 Eine vierstöckige Quergalerie verknüpft die drei Unterrichts-blöcke horizontal und vertikal; sie gibt den Blick in die verglaste Turnhalle und Aula frei, so daß die Schüler das Bauprinzip im Detail erkennen können.

4

1

2

3

1–2 Assembly hall.
  3 Classroom corridor. All services
    run in the corridor areas, leaving
    the main rooms as free as possible.
  4 Detail of gallery walkways.
    The spartan construction enforced
    by economical constraints is
    turned into straightforward
    structural clarity.
5–6 Entrance level below the galleries.
    The inclined glass wall separates
    the gymnasium from the main
    circulation spaces.
  7 View of gymnasium from the
    upper levels of the gallery.

1–2 Hall de réunion.
  3 Couloir desservant les salles de
    classes. Tous les vides techniques
    sont placés dans les couloirs
    libérant ainsi un maximum
    d'espace dans les salles principales.
  4 Détail des passerelles de la galerie.
    La construction spartiate imposée
    par les contraintes de budgets
    se traduit par une structure simple
    et claire.
5–6 Entrée au niveau inférieur aux
    galeries. Le mur en verre incliné
    sépare le gymnase des espaces
    de circulation.
  7 Vue du gymnase des niveaux
    supérieurs de la galerie.

1–2 Aula.
  3 Korridor vor den Klassenzimmern.
    Die gesamte Haustechnik verläuft
    in den Korridorbereichen, um die
    Haupträume so frei wie möglich
    zu halten.
  4 Detail der Galeriestege. Die
    spartanische Bauweise, durch
    Finanzierungszwänge bedingt,
    verwandelt sich in strukturelle
    Transparenz.
5–6 Eingangsebene unter den Galerien.
    Die schräge Glaswand trennt die
    Turnhalle von den Hauptverkehrs-
    räumen.
  7 Von den oberen Galerieebenen
    ein Blick in die Turnhalle.

4

5

6

7

1 Assembly hall. The large south-
facing spaces are efficiently
ventilated through a heat-recovery
system at the top.
2 Gymnasium.

1 Hall de réunion. Les salles
orientées vers le sud sont ventilées
grâce au système de récupération
de chaleur en hauteur.
2 Le gymnase.

1 Die Aula. Die großen Räume auf
der Südseite werden durch ein
Wärmerückgewinnungssystem
unter der Decke effizient belüftet.
2 Turnhalle.

1

2

1 Detail of east-facing vertical
 glazing and blinds.
2 Gallery.
3–4 Corridor in classroom block.
 Steel-mesh cabinets protect vertical
 services feeding the individual
 classrooms.
5,7 External terrace at entrance level.
6 View of the city past a ventilator
 shaft at the roof of the classroom
 block.

1 Détail du vitrage et des stores
 verticaux côté est.
2 Galerie.
3–4 Couloir du bloc des salles de
 classes. Les meubles en maille
 d'acier protègent les vides
 techniques verticaux qui
 alimentent les salles de classes.
5,7 Terrasse externe au niveau de
 l'entrée.
6 Vue de la ville par derrière une
 gaine de ventilation sur le toit
 du bloc des salles de classes.

1 Detailansicht der Vertikalver-
 glasung und Jalousien auf der
 Ostseite.
2 Galerie.
3–4 Korridor im Unterrichtsblock.
 Stahlsiebschränke schützen die
 vertikal verlaufende Haustechnik
 auf dem Weg in die Klassenzimmer.
5,7 Terrasse in Höhe der Eingang.
6 Blick auf die Stadt, vorbei an
 einem Belüftungsschacht auf dem
 Dach des Unterrichtsblocks.

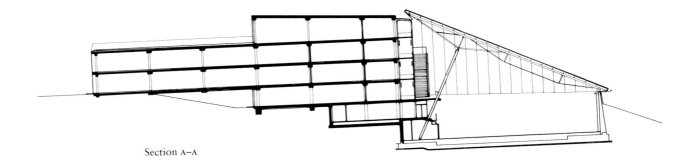

Section A–A

20 metres

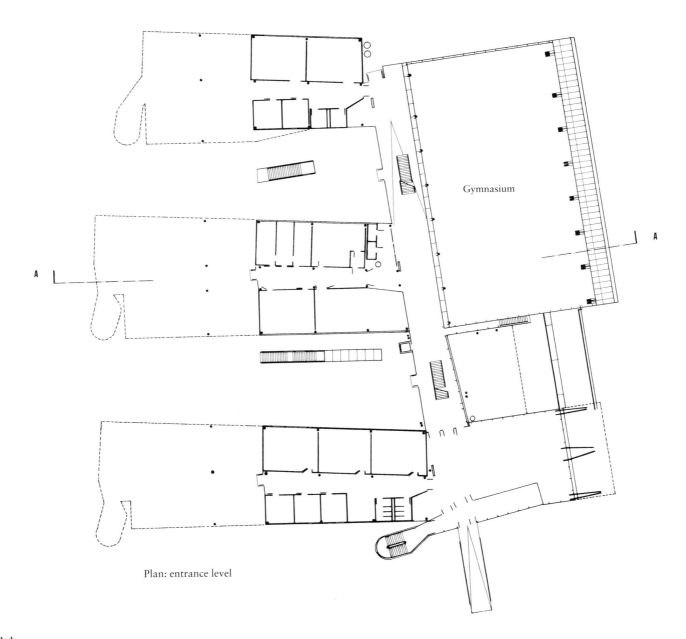

Gymnasium

A

A

Plan: entrance level

Site plan

Helmut Richter
1994

Address	Kinkplatz 21, 1014 Vienna
Client	Magistrat der Stadt Wien
Developer	GSD (Michael Wachberger)
Project team	Jakob Dunkl, Gerd Erhartt, Andreas Gerner, Heide Mehring
Main contractor	GSD (Hans Schwartz)
Structural engineer	Vasko & Partner (Lothar Heinrich)
Environmental engineer	Erich Panzhauser
Mechanical and electrical	Freudensprung Engineering
Steelwork	Binder & Co AG, Gleisdorf; Heidenbauer, Bruk/Mur
Metalwork	Wibeba, Vösendorf; L. Brandstätter, Frohnleiten; Völkl, Leoben; Profilstahl, Vienna
Glass façades	Eckelt + Co, Steyr
Precast concrete	Anzinger, Wels
Interiors	Kaefer, Vienna; IL-Bau, Klagenfurt
Finishes	Schmied, Vienna
Sunshading	Clauss, Zwölfaxing
Lighting	Knoblich, Vienna
Size	13,000 square metres
Construction cost	AS 18,000/net square metre

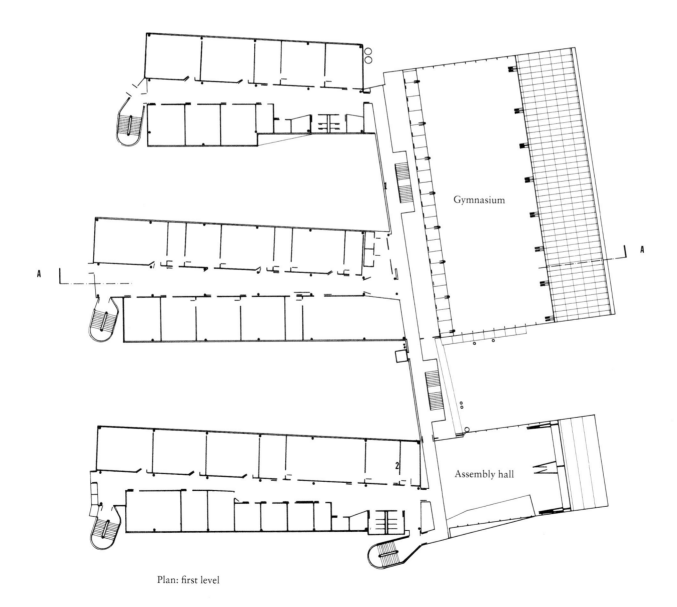

Plan: first level

It is unimaginable to have an architecture without context. Even unbuilt projects, paper architecture, are conceived within a framework of functions and priorities and are affected even by the paper on which they are printed. In the case of built architecture, the word 'context' usually refers to the building's immediate physical surroundings. These are, however, only one of the factors which determine the final appearance of a building: a more comprehensive definition of 'context' must include the specific set of circumstances which led, step by laborious step, to the building's physical construction.

'Context' is many things. The context of a building includes the self-image of the city, the personal ambitions of politicians, the visions of architects. Context is the grime which starts to soil the gleaming metal and glass of a new building the day after its construction is complete. Context is the newspaper article that appears in the following weekend supplement, praising or damning. Context is the sound of a door slamming, a tap dripping, a dog barking in a hallway five, ten, 50 years later. The context for the projects chosen for presentation in this book is this extended city: it is Vienna, its buildings, its politics, its people, its history and its psychology, its clients and its architects, its palaces and its pastries. If the projects have anything in common, it is the fact that they have placed themselves very consciously within the psyche of the city, either carefully, like the MAK-Café, or with bodice-ripping bravado, like the Kinkplatz School. All but two are located on or within the Ringstrasse, in the historic centre of Vienna, a dense environment studded with the emblems of the city's identity, and very closely protected. The MAK-Café is a subtle event within an existing monument. The SKALA-Bar offers a secret escape route from the city.

All the projects reflect the different talents and ambitions of the architects who designed them. Many factors have to work together to produce an exceptional building, and the architect's ambition and ability to create, to give form to communal concerns, is possibly the least significant of these factors, despite what architects themselves would like to think. Private money, public subsidies, site availability, planning policies, building regulations – all of these need to be in place before the architect is even invited to join the effort. And yet architects want so much. Lone heroes of truth and beauty engaged in a solitary battle against ignorance and populism, their desire to design not only fuels their own work, hour after hour of unpaid, unappreciated work, but creates a collective vision that is a continuous presence behind the fabric of the city. This architectonic will exerts a constant pressure that finds release only on the very few occasions where by various means a hole has been made through which architecture can be expressed. The talent of the architect lies not so much in the design of the glorious new edifice as in handling the endless process of negotiation

1 As part of their city-planning research, Eichinger oder Knechtl designed covers for *Falter*, Vienna's weekly events paper.
2 *Falter*, current cover design.
3–4 *re-print*, a selection of newspaper articles on architecture, art and science, republished by Eichinger oder Knechtl.

1 Dans le cadre de leur recherche urbanistique, Eichinger oder Knechtl ont dessiné la couverture du *Falter*.
2 Le *Falter*, dessin de la couverture actuelle.
3–4 *re-print*, sélection d'articles de journaux sur l'architecture, l'art et les sciences réédités par Eichinger oder Knechtl.

1 Im Rahmen ihrer Stadtplanungsforschung entwarfen Eichinger oder Knechtl Titelseiten für das Wiener Wochenmagazin *Falter*.
2 Aktuelle Titelgestaltung des *Falter*.
3–4 *re-print*, eine Auswahl von Zeitungsartikeln über Architektur, Kunst und Wissenschaft, neu aufgelegt von Eichinger oder Knechtl.

1   2

Il est impensable d'avoir une architecture sans contexte. Même si les projets non réalisés, à savoir l'architecture en deux dimensions, sont conçus selon un schéma qui tient compte des fonctions et priorités, ils ont aussi une incidence sur les plans sur lesquels ils sont tirés. En ce qui concerne l'architecture réalisée, le terme de «contexte» fait référence, en général, aux constructions dans son environnement immédiat. Mais ces dernières ne constituent qu'un facteur parmi d'autres qui détermine l'aspect final d'un bâtiment. Pour être complet, le terme de contexte doit comprendre un ensemble bien défini d'éléments qui ont abouti, petit à petit, à la construction effective du bâtiment. Le mot «contexte» englobe beaucoup de choses.

Architektur ohne Kontext ist unvorstellbar. Selbst theoretische Projekte werden innerhalb eines Rahmens bestimmter Funktionen und Prioritäten konzipiert und sogar von dem Papier beeinflußt, auf dem sie gedruckt sind. Bei existierenden Gebäuden bezieht sich das Wort »Kontext« gewöhnlich auf die unmittelbare Umgebung des Baus. Das ist aber nur einer der Faktoren, die das endgültige Aussehen eines Gebäudes bestimmen; eine umfassendere Definition von «Kontext» muß die genauen Umstände enthalten, die langsam, Schritt für Schritt, zu der Errichtung des Gebäudes geführt haben. »Kontext« kann viele Dinge bedeuten. Der Kontext eines Gebäudes beinhaltet das Selbstverständnis der Stadt, die persönlichen Ambitionen der Politiker, die Phantasie der Architekten. Kontext bedeutet aber auch den Schmutz, der das glänzende Metall und Glas eines neuen Gebäudes schon gleich nach seiner Fertigstellung zu verunzieren beginnt. Kontext bedeutet die Presseartikel, die das neue Gebäude in der nächsten Wochenendausgabe bejubeln oder verreißen. Kontext – das ist das Geräusch einer zuschlagenden Tür, eines tropfenden Wasserhahns, des Hundegebells in einem Korridor, fünf, zehn, fünfzig Jahre später. Der Kontext der für die Aufnahme in das vorliegende Buch gewählten Projekte ist diese erweiterte Stadt: Wien, seine Gebäude, seine Politik, seine Menschen, seine Geschichte und Psychologie, seine Bauherren und Architekten, seine Paläste und seine Mehlspeisen. Wenn die Projekte irgend etwas gemeinsam haben, dann ist es die Tatsache, daß sie sich sehr deutlich in der Psyche der Stadt verwurzelt haben – entweder vorsichtig, wie das MAK-Café, oder mit draufgängerischer Bravour, wie die Schule Kinkplatz. Mit zwei Ausnahmen liegen sie alle an oder innerhalb der Ringstraße, im historischen Zentrum Wiens, einer dichten kleinen Welt, gespickt mit Identitäts-Emblemen der Stadt und sorgsam geschützt. Das MAK-Café ist ein subtiles Ereignis in einem bestehenden Baudenkmal; SKALA-Bar und Restaurant bieten einen geheimen Fluchtweg aus der Stadt.

Alle diese Projekte reflektieren die verschiedenen Talente und Ambitionen ihrer Architekten. Viele Faktoren müssen zusammenkommen, um ein außergewöhnliches Gebäude entstehen zu lassen – und die Ambitionen und Fähigkeiten des Architekten,

3

Contexts

Le contexte d'un bâtiment comprend l'image que la ville veut se donner, l'ambition personnelle des hommes politiques, la représentation des architectes. Le contexte, c'est la saleté qui commence à ternir les métaux reluisants et à voiler les vitres transparentes d'un nouvel immeuble, le lendemain de sa livraison. Le contexte, c'est l'article élogieux ou accablant qui paraîtra dans le prochain supplément du week-end. Le contexte, c'est le bruit d'une porte qui claque, d'un robinet qui goutte, d'un chien qui aboie dans un couloir cinq ans, dix ans, 50 ans plus tard.

Le contexte choisi pour ce livre, c'est cette ville étendue, c'est Vienne avec ses bâtiments, sa politique, ses habitants, son histoire et sa psychologie, ses maîtres

d'oeuvre et d'ouvrage, ses palais et ses gâteaux. Si les projets ont quelque chose en commun, c'est peut-être parce qu'ils ont été attentivement intégrés dans la psyché de la ville, avec une grande précaution dans le cas du café MAK, avec beaucoup de culot dans le cas de l'École Kinkplatz. Presque tous sont situés sur la Ringstrasse ou dans son enceinte, le centre historique très dense et sauvegardé de Vienne, couvert d'emblèmes à l'image de la ville. Le café du MAK est une intervention subtile à l'intérieur d'un monument existant. Le bar-restaurant SKALA est un havre de paix au milieu de la ville.

Tout ces projets reflètent les différents talents et ambitions des architectes qui les ont conçus. Plusieurs facteurs doivent être réunis pour réaliser un bâtiment

d'exception et l'ambition de l'architecte ainsi que sa capacité à concevoir et répondre aux problèmes de la communauté font probablement partie des facteurs les moins importants, en dépit de ce que les architectes aiment à penser. L'argent du secteur privé, les subventions publiques, la disponibilité d'un site, les politiques urbanistiques, la législation relative à la construction, autant d'éléments qui doivent être réunis avant que l'architecte ne soit invité à entrer dans la danse. Et pourtant les architectes en veulent tellement. Héros incompris et solitaires, défenseurs de la vérité et de la beauté, engagés dans une bataille contre l'ignorance et la démagogie, leur désir de concevoir nourrit non seulement leur propre travail, si peu reconnu et fait de longues

heures non payées, mais il crée aussi une représentation collective qui est une présence permanente dans le tissu de la ville. Cette volonté architectonique ne s'assouvit que lorsque l'on donne à l'architecture le moyen de s'exprimer, quelles qu'en soient les manières.

Les talents de l'architecte ne résident pas tant dans la conception de nouveaux édifices glorieux, mais plutôt dans un processus de négociation sans fin qui permet au bâtiment d'être réalisé : c'est ce processus qui, pour finir, donne forme à l'objet construit. C'est grâce à cette patience en matière de négociation que Rüdiger Lainer a finalement pu construire son toit sur un immeuble situé dans le centre-ville protégé. C'est grâce à des discussions sur le budget que

etwas zu schaffen, den Anliegen der Gemeinschaft Form zu geben, haben dabei wahrscheinlich nebenrangige Bedeutung, gleich, was die Architekten selbst glauben mögen. Private und öffentliche Gelder, Baustellenverfügbarkeit, Planungsbestimmungen, Bauvorschriften – all das muß geregelt sein, noch ehe der Architekt überhaupt verpflichtet wird. Aber trotzdem wollen die Architekten so viel. Diese einsamen Helden der Wahrheit und Schönheit, die allein ihren Kampf gegen Ignoranz und Populismus führen und deren Verlangen zu zeichnen nicht nur ihre eigene Tätigkeit vorantreibt – viele Stunden unbezahlter, eigentlich nie gewürdigter Arbeit –, sondern dann auch eine kollektive Vision schafft, die als kontinuierliche Präsenz hinter dem Gefüge der Stadt steht. Dieser architek-

4

through which a building project is realised: it is this process which finally shapes the built object. It was patient negotiation which allowed Rüdiger Lainer to build on the rooftop in the protected city centre. It was financial arguments which enabled Helmut Richter to opt for a steel-braced structure rather than rendered mass concrete for his school. These areas, more than the design itself, require the application of the architect's imagination, in order to coax the camel through the eye of the needle, to smuggle architecture past the border guards of reality.

A new building is brutal, it is shocking. It pokes a hole in city life. It forces people to change their habits, to take new routes, to look elsewhere to see the sky. It forces their bodies into contact with new materials: they must walk on new stones, hear their voices thrown back from new surfaces, meet their own eyes in new mirrors. And it forces them into contact with each other: across new counters, pressed together in new lifts, walking new corridors, facing strangers at new tables. This new hole in reality, before it starts to heal over, covered by the scar tissue of new habits, of dust and dirt, briefly lets in light and fresh air through the heavy blanket of normality. Before it is conquered by familiarity, it represents unknown dreams, new possibilities, it prises open and challenges preconceptions. It may even provide an escape from the unbearable city in which it is located.

Once a building is built, it cannot be undone: it is part of public life, and even if it is physically demolished, it is still part of public memory, an indelible scar on reality. For a brief moment the terrifying beast of the city has been stalled; diverted by a sharp reflection, the bright gleam of an architect's vision. For a moment, in the planes and angles of a new building, in bronze and in brass, in the imprints in concrete and in finely polished wood, the suffering city can see reflected a vision of its body healed. And inch by painful inch, even as the new buildings become worn and dull, the city grows, not only in circumference but from the inside, slowly: with each new coat of paint, each leaking roof repaired, as well as each new design that helps to expand the boundaries of what buildings can do, what architecture can be, what is possible in a city.

1 Bus stop, bird house on wheels.
2 Bird house.

1 Arrêt de bus, cage à oiseau sur roue.
2 Cage à oiseau.

1 Bushaltestelle, Vogelhaus auf Rädern.
2 Vogelhaus.

1

tonische Wille übt einen ständigen Druck aus, der sich nur bei den wenigen Gelegenheiten aufhebt, wenn es gelingt, auf irgendwelche Weise ein »Loch« zu öffnen, durch das die Architektur ihren Ausdruck finden kann. Das Talent des Architekten liegt weniger im Entwurf eines glorreichen neuen Gebäudes als in der Bewältigung des endlosen Verhandlungsverfahrens, durch das ein Bauprojekt schließlich verwirklicht wird. Dieses Verfahren ist es, das letztlich das zu bauende Objekt formt. Geduldige Verhandlungen waren es, die es Rüdiger Lainer schließlich gestatteten, auf einem Dach im geschützten Stadtzentrum zu bauen; finanzielle Argumente waren es, die es Helmut Richter ermöglichten, sich bei seinem Schulgebäude für eine Stahlskelettstruktur zu entscheiden anstatt für Anwurf mit Massenbeton. Das sind die Gebiete, die noch mehr als der Entwurf selbst die Vorstellungskraft des Architekten erfordern – um das Kamel durch das Nadelöhr zu treiben, um Architektur an den Grenzwächtern der Realität vorbeischmuggeln zu können.

Ein neues Gebäude ist brutal, schockierend. Es bohrt eine Öffnung in das Leben der Stadt, es zwingt Menschen dazu, ihre Gewohnheiten zu ändern, neue Wege zu finden, dort zu stehen, wo sie zu sitzen pflegten, anderswo hinzuschauen, um den Himmel sehen zu können. Ein neues Gebäude zwingt ihre Körper in Berührung mit neuen Materialien: Sie müssen über einen neuen Steinboden gehen und hören, wie ihre Stimmen von neuen Wänden zurückgeworfen werden, sie sehen ihre Augen in neuen Spiegeln. Und neue Gebäude zwingen die Menschen auch zu neuen Kontakten miteinander: über neue Ladentische und Theken hinweg, zusammengedrängt in neuen Aufzügen, beim Gehen durch neue Korridore, beim Sitzen mit Fremden an neuen Tischen. Bevor dann diese neue Öffnung in der Realität wieder heilt, geschlossen wird von den Narben neuer Gewohnheiten und von Staub und Schmutz, läßt es für kurze Zeit Licht und frische Luft durch die schwere Decke des Alltags ein. Bevor diese Öffnung wieder von Gewöhnung normalisiert wird, repräsentiert sie unbekannte Träume und neue Möglichkeiten, rüttelt an vorgefaßten Meinungen; sie mag sogar einen Fluchtweg aus der unerträglichen Stadt bieten, in die sie gebohrt wurde.

Sobald ein Bauwerk errichtet ist, kann es

2

Helmut Richter a pu construire, pour son école, une charpente contreventée plutôt qu'une masse en béton enduite. Ce sont ces étapes plutôt que la conception elle-même qui exigent de l'architecte une imagination pertinente pour réaliser l'impossible et faire passer l'architecture de l'autre côté de la réalité et de ses frontières protégées.

Un nouvel immeuble, c'est toujours violent, toujours dérangeant. Cela fait une marque dans la vie de la ville. Cela contraint les gens à changer leurs habitudes, à emprunter de nouvelles routes, à être debout là où ils étaient assis, à regarder le ciel d'un autre point de vue. Cela oblige leur corps à se confronter à de nouveaux matériaux : ils se voient forcés de marcher sur de nouvelles pierres, d'entendre l'écho de leur voix renvoyée sur de nouvelles surfaces et de croiser leur propre regard dans de nouveaux miroirs. Et cela les contraint à rencontrer l'autre en de nouveaux lieux, à être pressés dans de nouveaux ascenseurs, à arpenter de nouveaux couloirs, à être assis à côté d'étrangers à de nouvelles tables. Avant qu'elle ne se referme, cette blessure dans la réalité, pansée par les habitudes nouvelles, la poussière et la saleté, laisse un bref instant passer l'air et la lumière à travers l'épaisse couche de la normalité. Avant de devenir familière, cette blessure incarne des rêves inconnus, des possibilités nouvelles, force et défie les idées préconçues. Elle peut même servir de fuite hors de la ville insupportable dans laquelle elle se trouve. Une fois qu'un bâtiment est construit, il ne peut être détruit. Il fait partie de la vie de la ville et, même si on le démolit, il n'en reste pas moins partie intégrante de la mémoire collective, une cicatrice ineffaçable sur la réalité. Pendant un court instant, l'effrayante bête de la ville est maîtrisée et détournée de sa proie par une étincelle, la lueur vive de la vision d'un architecte. L'espace d'un instant, sur les plans et les angles d'un nouvel immeuble, sur le bronze et le cuivre, sur l'empreinte en béton et en bois admirablement poli, la ville souffrante peut entrevoir l'image d'un corps guéri. Et douloureusement, centimètre par centimètre, même si les nouveaux bâtiments passent et deviennent ennuyeux, la ville grandit, non seulement en taille mais aussi de l'intérieur, doucement : chaque couche de peinture, chaque fuite de toit réparée, ainsi que chaque nouvel élément qui aide à repousser les frontières de ce que les bâtiments peuvent faire, de ce que l'architecture peut être, de ce qui est possible dans une ville.

nicht mehr »unwirklich« gemacht werden; es ist Teil des öffentlichen Lebens, und selbst wenn es zerstört wird, bleibt es doch im Gedächtnis der Öffentlichkeit bestehen, eine ewige Narbe an der Realität. Für einen kurzen Augenblick ist das furchterregende Untier namens »Stadt« aufgehalten worden; der Drache wurde vielleicht nicht erlegt, aber zumindest vorübergehend irritiert – abgelenkt durch ein scharfes Bild, den hellen Glanz der Vision eines Architekten. Für einen Augenblick kann die leidende Stadt in den Ebenen und Winkeln eines neuen Gebäudes, in Bronze und Messing, in Formen aus Beton und schön poliertem Holz das Abbild einer Vision ihres geheilten Körpers erkennen. Unter Schmerzen, Zentimeter um Zentimeter, während die neuen Gebäude ebenfalls abgenutzt und stumpf werden, wächst die Stadt: nicht nur dem Umfang nach, sondern langsam auch von innen her, mit jedem neuen Farbanstrich, mit jedem reparierten Dach, mit jedem Element, das mithilft, die Grenzen baulicher, architektonischer Möglichkeiten zu erweitern – die Grenzen der Möglichkeiten einer Stadt.

Urban practices

Eichinger oder Knechtl

The modern city, the purpose of which is to give you everything, simultaneously denies you the comfort of universal truth, authority, the right answer. The resulting contradictions are intolerable, particularly in a city which still relies on its imperial past to give meaning to its physicality. In the context of the Austrian capital, the work of Gregor Eichinger and Christian Knechtl is a survival strategy. They grab hold of anything they can and examine it, knead it, look at it quizzically, then throw it away to grab hold of the next thing, like children, unimpeded by the pathetic heroism which frustrates so many other ambitious architects. They take part in the city they live in, they give it (or try their damnedest to give it) their books, projects, places, buildings, parties, visions, thoughts.

Gregor Eichinger organises techno-parties, and the duo have done book designs and the cover for the *Falter*, Vienna's weekly events paper, all of which they consider essential parts of their city-planning research. They do exhibition designs for others but are also working on curating their own exhibition, on turbulence. They have just released their own publication entitled *re-print*, which presents articles and images on architecture, science and art which they have collected and consider too good to be lost when the newspaper which carried them becomes waste paper. In a city where the architectural profession is easily lost in self-congratulation, Eichinger oder Knechtl present a constant irreverent challenge. If architectural projects make holes in reality, theirs is a machine-gun practice: the two projects presented here are not necessarily representative of their overall production, but are simply the two latest ones.

JEWISH MUSEUM The construction of a new Jewish Museum in the middle of Vienna, just off the Graben, the main tourist shopping street, is an important addition to the city. The search for a permanent place for the Max Berger collection of Jewish religious artefacts, denied a home since the Nazi destruction of the previous Jewish Museum in 1938, was one of the expressed concerns of Vienna's former mayor, Helmut Zilk. A museum was finally opened in the early nineteenth-century Palais Eskeles.

Eichinger oder Knechtl's contribution, following an invited competition in 1995, is to reorganise the old palace to house a museum not only for Jewish religion and history but for the exhibition of contemporary Viennese Jewish culture. The inner courtyard has been roofed over by a curved glass roof to become the main room: an empty space, housing only the small but very valuable Berger collection. There is also a new bookshop, café and ticket kiosk. The two upper floors are connected to the main space by open galleries through which you can see the

La ville moderne est là pour vous offrir tout ce qui existe mais, simultanément, elle vous refuse le confort de la vérité universelle et du pouvoir ou de toute réponse adéquate. Les contradictions qui en résultent sont intolérables. Elles le sont encore davantage dans cette ville qui invoque son passé impérial pour justifier son aspect actuel. Dans le contexte qu'est celui de la capitale autrichienne, le travail de Gregor Eichinger et Christian Knechtl est une vraie stratégie de survie. Ils s'emparent de tout ce qu'ils trouvent, le retournent, le regardent perplexes puis le jettent et saisissent un autre objet. Ils sont comme des enfants, dépourvus d'un quelconque héroisme pitoyable, celui dont souffrent tant d'architectes ambitieux. Ils participent à la ville dans laquelle ils vivent et lui donnent (ou du moins font tout leur possible pour lui donner) leurs livres, leurs projets, leurs places, leurs immeubles, leurs fêtes, leurs visions, leurs pensées. Gregor Eichinger organise des fêtes technos. Lui et Christian Knechtl ont aussi dessiné des maquettes de livre et la couverture du *Falter*, l'hebdomadaire des spectacles et événements de Vienne. Pour eux, ces diverses activités sont des éléments essentiels de leur recherche urbanistique. Ils ont réalisé la scénographie de plusieurs expositions et travaillent actuellement sur leur propre exposition, dont le thème est la turbulence. Leur propre publication, intitulée *re-print*, vient de paraître et présente des articles et des images sur l'architecture, la science et les arts qu'ils ont choisis et qu'ils considèrent comme trop importants pour terminer à la poubelle une fois lus. Dans une ville où les architectes s'adonnent facilement à l'autosatisfaction, l'agence Eichinger oder Knechtl ne manque jamais de lancer des défis insolents. Si les réalisations architecturales sont des blessures dans la réalité, leur agence est une mitraillette : les deux projets choisis pour cet ouvrage ne sont pas nécessairement représentatifs de l'ensemble de leur travail. Ils sont tout simplement les derniers projets qu'ils ont réalisés.

LE MUSÉE D'HISTOIRE JUIVE La construction d'un musée d'histoire juive gleich neben dem Graben, einer der wichtigsten Einkaufsstraßen für Touristen, stellt eine bedeutende Bereicherung der Stadt dar. Die Suche nach einem permanenten Heim für die Max-Berger-Sammlung jüdischer Artefakte und Memorabilien, die seit der Zerstörung des früheren Jüdischen Museums durch die Nationalsozialisten im Jahr 1938 obdachlos war, war ein großes Anliegen des früheren Wiener Bürgermeisters Helmut Zilk. Das neue Museum wurde schließlich im Palais Eskeles aus dem 19. Jahrhundert eröffnet.

Die moderne Stadt, deren Zweck es ist, einem alles zu geben, versagt einem gleichzeitig den Trost der universellen Wahrheit, der Autorität, der richtigen Antwort. Die daraus erwachsenden Widersprüche sind unerträglich, besonders in einer Stadt, die sich immer noch auf ihre kaiserliche Vergangenheit verläßt, um ihrer heutigen Gestalt einen Sinn zu geben. Im Kontext der österreichischen Hauptstadt ist die Arbeit von Gregor Eichinger und Christian Knechtl eine Überlebensstrategie. Sie greifen auf, was sie nur können, um es zu untersuchen, kneten es durch, betrachten es forschend und werfen es wieder fort, um sich dem nächsten Ding zuzuwenden – wie Kinder, unbelastet von dem jämmerlichen Heroismus, der so viele andere ehrgeizige Architekten frustriert. Sie nehmen teil an der Stadt, in der sie leben, sie geben ihr (oder versuchen das doch mit aller Gewalt) ihre Bücher, Projekte, Gebäude, Parties, Visionen und Gedanken.

Gregor Eichinger organisiert Techno-Parties, und Knechtl und er haben Buchumschläge und Titelseiten für das Wiener Wochenmagazin *Falter* entworfen – alles Aktivitäten, die sie als wesentliche Bestandteile ihrer Stadtplanungsforschung betrachten. Sie fertigen Ausstellungsentwürfe für andere an, arbeiten aber auch an einer eigenen Ausstellung – über Turbulenz. Eichinger und Knechtl haben gerade selbst eine Publikation mit dem Titel *re-print* herausgebracht, die Artikel und Bilder über Architektur, Wissenschaft und Kunst enthält – Artikel, die sie gesammelt haben und für zu wichtig halten, als sie zusammen mit den Zeitungen, in denen sie erschienen, zu Makulatur werden zu lassen. In einer Stadt, in der sich das Architekturgewerbe allzu leicht in Selbstgefälligkeit ergeht, stellen Eichinger und Knechtl so etwas wie einen konstanten, irritierenden Juckreiz dar. Wenn architektonische Projekte Öffnungen in die Realität machen, dann schießen diese beiden Männer mit dem Maschinengewehr. Ihre hier präsentierten Projekte sind nicht unbedingt typisch für ihr Gesamtwerk, sondern lediglich ihre jüngsten Arbeiten.

JÜDISCHES MUSEUM Der Bau eines neuen jüdischen Museums im Herzen Wiens, Der nach einem Wettbewerb im Jahre 1995 von Eichinger oder Knechtl erbetene Beitrag bestand darin, das alte Palais so umzubauen, daß es nicht nur ein Museum für jüdische Religion und Geschichte auf-

dark moulded wood of the original panelled ceilings. Right at the top the main bulk of the religious objects in the museum's collection is kept in an accessible depot, massed together in a glass cube glimmering with silver. The main room, visible from the street though guarded by metal detectors, adds another public space to the city centre: after almost 60 years, it is a first cautious invitation giving the Austrian public a view into Jewish culture.

FIRST FLOOR The famous Mounier Bar on the Kärntnerstrasse, frequented by the artists and writers of the 1930s, was recently demolished, and pieces of the old interior were waiting to be thrown out when Michael Satke saw them and bought them. Eichinger oder Knechtl have reused them to complete Satke's complex of bars in the Rabensteig. The old interior panelling and furniture are combined with new materials in a recycling project which makes the single-room bar look as if it has already been there for 30 years, but is still waiting for something new to happen. The entrance is across a piece of glass floor and through a small mirrored cell. The effect is disorienting, as if you have entered an ancient spaceship on its way to places far from Vienna. Go there after dark, when the only light comes through the two large aquariums behind the bar: the First Floor is a pocket carved out of the city, a finely crafted fabrication.

en plein centre, à quelques pas du Graben, est une contribution importante à la ville de Vienne. L'une des priorités de Helmut Zilk, l'ancien maire de Vienne, a été la recherche d'un lieu qui puisse accueillir la collection d'objets religieux juifs de Max Berger, sans résidence depuis la destruction du Musée d'Histoire Juive par les Nazis en 1938. C'est finalement dans le Palais Eskeles de la fin 19ème siècle que s'ouvrira le musée.

Lauréats en 1995 du concours invité, Eichinger oder Knechtl ont dû réorganiser l'ancien palais pour y accueillir non seulement un musée de l'histoire et de la religion juive mais aussi un espace d'exposition de la culture juive contemporaine à Vienne. La cour intérieure est recouverte d'un toit en verre convexe qui devient la salle principale : un espace vierge qui expose uniquement la petite mais précieuse collection de Max Berger. Ils ont aussi aménagé une librairie, un café et une billetterie. Les deux étages supérieurs sont reliés à l'espace principal par des galeries ouvertes à travers lesquelles on peut voir les moulures en bois noir des panneaux du plafond d'origine. Au dernier étage, la plupart des objets religieux de la collection du musée sont réunis dans une pièce-dépôt accessible et l'argent des pièces exposées sous verre brille à nouveau. La salle principale, protégée par des détecteurs de métaux, est visible de la rue et constitue un nouvel espace public pour le centre-ville. Quelque 60 ans plus tard, les Autrichiens sont, enfin, gentiment invités à découvrir la culture juive.

FIRST FLOOR On a récemment démoli le célèbre bar Mounier de la Kärntnerstrasse qui était fréquenté par les artistes et écrivains des années 30. On était sur le point de jeter les pièces de son intérieur lorsque Michael Satke les découvrent et les rachètent. Eichinger oder Knechtl les ont ensuite recyclées pour terminer l'ensemble des bars de Satke sur la Rabensteig. Les panneaux et meubles de l'ancien intérieur ont été assemblés à des matériaux neufs dans un projet de recyclage qui donne au bar l'aspect d'un lieu qui a plus de trente ans mais qui attend toujours que quelque chose de nouveau se produise. En haut des escaliers ouverts, se trouve l'entrée que l'on franchit après avoir traversé un sol en verre et une petite cabine recouverte de miroirs. Le résultat est déroutant, c'est un peu comme si l'on pénétrait dans un vieux vaisseau spatial, en route pour une destination loin de Vienne. Allez-y après la tombée de la nuit quand la seule et unique lumière est celle qui est diffusée par les deux immenses aquariums posés derrière le bar. Le First Floor est une entaille dans la ville, une petite oeuvre d'art.

nehmen kann, sondern auch eine Ausstellung zeitgenössischer jüdischer Kultur. Der Innenhof wurde mit einem gebogenen Glasdach überdeckt und wurde zum Hauptsaal: ein leerer Riesenraum, der lediglich die kleine, aber höchst wertvolle Max-Berger-Sammlung beherbergt. Ferner gibt es eine neue Buchhandlung, ein Kaffeehaus und einen Kiosk für den Kartenverkauf. Die beiden oberen Stockwerke sind mit dem Hauptsaal durch offene Galerien verbunden, durch die man die dunkle Holztäfelung der Originaldecke sehen kann. Ganz oben wird die große Mehrheit der religiösen Objekte dieser Sammlung in einem leicht zugänglichen Depot aufbewahrt – in einem großen, silbrig schimmernden Glaswürfel. Der von der Straße aus sichtbare Hauptsaal – durch Metalldetektoren gesichert – verleiht dem Stadtzentrum wieder einen neuen, öffentlichen Blickpunkt: Nach fast 60 Jahren ist es die erste, vorsichtige Einladung an die Österreicher, Einblick in die jüdische Kultur zu gewinnen.

FIRST FLOOR Die berühmte Mounier-Bar in der Kärntner Straße, in den dreißiger Jahren Treffpunkt von Künstlern und Schriftstellern, wurde vor einiger Zeit abgerissen; manche Innenteile und Einrichtungsgegenstände warteten auf die Müllabfuhr, als Michael Satke sie entdeckte und aufkaufte. Eichinger oder Knechtl haben diese Elemente nun bei der Fertigstellung von Satkes Barkomplex am Rabensteig eingesetzt. Die alte Möbel der Mounier-Bar wurden mit neuen Materialien in einem Recycling-Projekt kombiniert, das die neue Einraum-Bar so aussehen läßt, als ob es sie schon seit mindestens 30 Jahren dort gäbe, aber doch irgendwie auf etwas Neues wartete. Der Eingang führt über einen Glasboden und durch eine kleine Spiegelzelle. Der Effekt ist verwirrend – man glaubt, in ein uraltes Raumschiff einzudringen, für das Wien nur noch eine Erinnerung auf dem Weg ins weite All ist. Gehen Sie nach Einbruch der Dunkelheit dorthin, wenn die einzige Beleuchtung von den zwei großen Aquarien hinter der Bar ausgeht; First Floor ist eine kleine, in die Stadt eingeschnitzte Nische – eine liebevoll ausgearbeitete Erfindung.

1–2 View through the entrance of Palais Eskeles to the new covered courtyard at the back.
3 Third-floor museum depot.
4 The inner courtyard with the Berger collection.
5 Detail of the curved glazed steel canopy covering the rear yard. A permanent translucent blind filters the light. The murals are by Nancy Spero.
6 Detail of the glass case housing the Max Berger collection, with quotes from Jewish liturgy.

1–2 Vue de l'entrée du Palais Eskeles de la cour couverte, située à l'arrière.
3 Pièce-dépôt au troisième étage du musée.
4 La cour intérieure avec la collection Berger.
5 Détail du auvent courbe vitré à la structure en acier qui couvre la cour, située à l'arrière. Un store translucide permanent filtre la lumière. Fresques de Nancy Spero.
6 Détail de la vitrine renfermant la collection Max Berger avec des citations de la liturgie juive.

1–2 Blick durch den Eingang des Palais Eskeles auf den neuen, über-deckten Hof auf der Rückseite.
3 Museumsdepot im 3. Stock.
4 Der Innenhof mit der Berger-Sammlung.
5 Detailansicht des gebogenen Glas-Stahl-Dachs über dem hinteren Hof. Das einfallende Licht wird von einer Blende gefiltert. Die Wandmalereien stammen von Nancy Spero.
6 Detail des Glaswürfels, der die Max-Berger-Sammlung beher-bergt, mit Zitaten aus der jü-dischen Liturgie.

Eichinger oder Knechtl
1995

Address Palais Eskeles, Dorotheergasse 11,
1010 Vienna

Client Jewish Museum of Vienna
GesmbH

Project team Gregor Eichinger, Christian
Knechtl, Andi Breuss, Büro Sam

Main contractor EKAZENT Bautenverwaltung
GesmbH

Mechanical and electrical IKM GesmbH

Glass roof Ferroglas

Joinery Fa. Waldbauer

Terrazzo Miromentwerk

Display cases Rothstein

Architect for the hologram installation Martin Kohlbauer

Mural Nancy Spero

Size 2250 square metres

Construction cost AS 30 million

5

6

1

1, 3 At night, almost all light to the room comes through the two large aquariums behind the bar.
2 Painting from the Mounier Bar. The architects have recycled an old interior, practising their own brand of city ecology.

1, 3 Le soir, presque tout l'éclairage de la pièce provient des deux grands aquariums situés derrière le bar.
2 Peinture du bar Mounier. Les architectes ont recyclé un ancien intérieur, mettant en application leur version de l'écologie urbaine.

1, 3 Nachts wird der Raum fast nur durch das Licht aus den beiden großen Aquarien hinter der Bar beleuchtet.
2 Gemälde in der Mounier-Bar. Die Architekten haben ein altes Interieur einem Recycling-Projekt zugeführt – ganz im Sinne ihrer eigenen Stadtökologie.

2

Eichinger oder Knechtl
1994
Address Seitenstettengasse 1, 1010 Vienna
Client Michael Satke
Project team Gregor Eichinger, Christian
Knechtl, Andi Breuss, Büro Sam
Mechanical and electrical Ing. Grainer + Partner OEG
Joinery Fa. Waldbauer
Aquarium Werner Knapp
Size 130 square metres

3

Rüdiger Lainer

Born 1949
Education Studied physics, sociology and painting in Vienna and Paris 1968–71; studied architecture at the TU Vienna 1970–8
Work Research on urban development and urban sociology 1978–83; Atelier Schwanzer 1984–6; established current practice 1986
Major projects Waidhausenstrasse housing, Vienna 1989–91
Office redevelopment, Hermanngasse, Vienna 1990
Aspern Siegesplatz housing, Vienna 1990–1
Rothenburgstrasse housing, Vienna 1990–
Absberggasse school, Vienna 1993–4
Edelsinnstrasse housing, Vienna 1993–5
Urban design project, Altes Flugfeld Aspern, 1993–
DESARTE: study of the emergence of new design practices encompassing art, technology and everyday culture 1995
Schießstätte housing, Graz 1996–
Production facility, Austria Email, Vienna 1996–
Publications *Austria: Architektur im 20. Jahrhundert*, Prestel 1995; Frank Dimster, *New Austrian Architecture*, Rizzoli 1995; Ramesh Biswas (ed), *Innovative Austrian Architecture 96*, Springer 1996

Hermann Czech

Education Studied under Konrad Wachsmann and Ernst A. Plischke
Work Established current practice 1961; visiting professor Hochschule für Angewandte Kunst, Vienna 1985–6; visiting professor Harvard University, US 1993–4
Major projects Haus s, Vienna 1980–3
Palais Schwarzenberg remodelling, Vienna 1982–4
Pedestrian bridge, Vienna Stadtpark 1985–7
Petrusgasse housing, Vienna 1985–9
Planning scheme for Vienna Underground 1985–9
Vienna Opera loggia glazing, 1991–4
Rosa Jochmann-Schule, Vienna 1991–4
Bank Austria head office remodelling, Vienna 1992–
Urban planning scheme, Oranienburg, Berlin, Germany 1992–3
Brunnergasse housing, Vienna 1994
Paltaufgasse housing, Vienna 1995–
Exhibition design 'Von Hier Aus', Düsseldorf 1984
'Wien 1938', Vienna 1988
'Wunderblock', Vienna 1989
Prizes City of Vienna award for architecture 1985
Exhibitions 'Hermann Czech', Architekturmuseum Basel, Switzerland 1996
Publications *Das Looshaus* (with Wolfgang Mistelbauer), Vienna 1976; 'The Diction of Otto Wagner', *A + U* (7/77); 'The Loos Idea', *A + U* (5/78); 'No Need for Panic', *A New Wave of Austrian Architecture*, Catalogue 13, IAUS New York 1980; 'A Mode for the Current Interpretation of Josef Frank', *A + U* (11/91); Pieter Jan Gijsberts, 'Architectuur als achtergrond: Theorie en werk van Hermann Czech', *de Architect* (11/90)

Biographies

Driendl & Steixner

Born	Georg Driendl 1956
	Gerhard Steixner 1953
Education	Akademie der bildenden Künste, Vienna
Work	Established current practice 1983
Major projects	Bogner apartment, Vienna 1988
	Haus Magerl 1989
	Invisible Shop, Vienna 1990
	Mariahilferstrasse offices, Vienna 1993
	Österreichische Schule, Budapest, Hungary 1994–
	Zinckgasse school, Vienna 1994–5
	Haus Furrer 1995–
Prizes	City of Vienna award for experimental architecture 1990; ÖKO prize for architecture 1991
Exhibitions	'The Gate of the Present', Rotterdam 1992; 'Architettura & Natura', Turin 1994; 'Innovative Austrian Architecture', Vienna 1996
Publications	*Ambiente* (1–2/95); Frank Dimster, *New Austrian Architecture*, Rizzoli 1995
Film and video	*Trans* (71 min, 16 mm) 1983; *Roland Rainer* (24 min, 16 mm) 1985; *Pause* (4 min, 16 mm) 1987; *Magic Wall* (3 min, video) 1991; *Standard Solar* (3 min, 35 mm/video) 1992

Helmut Richter

Born	1941
Education	TU Graz, graduated 1968; Paris, France 1968–9; UCLA, Los Angeles, US 1969–71
Work	Professor of architecture Ecole Nationale Supérieure des Beaux Arts, Paris, France 1971–5; lecturer Hochschule für angewandte Kunst, Vienna 1986–; visiting professor Gesamthochschule Kassel, Germany 1986–7; professor TU Vienna 1991–; established current practice 1977
Major projects	Mechanical furniture 1968
	Plattner House, Sollenau 1980
	Königseder House, Baumgartenberg 1980
	Gräf und Stift housing, Vienna 1981
	Kiang restaurant, Vienna 1984
	Brunnerstrasse housing, Vienna 1986–90
	Autofabrikstrasse housing, Vienna 1986–90
	Moto-Kawasaki factory, Vienna 1992
	Waidhausenstrasse school, Vienna 1995
Exhibition design	'Bildlicht – Malerei zwischen Material und Immaterialität', Vienna 1991; 'Die vertriebene Vernunft', Venice Biennale 1993
Prizes	City of Vienna award for architecture 1992

Eichinger oder Knechtl

Born	Gregor Eichinger 1956
	Christian Knechtl 1954
Education	Studied architecture in Vienna
Work	Established current practice 1981
Major projects	Conversion of a motel into an arts centre (with Bepi Maggiori and Marco Zanuso Jr), Burgenland 1982
	Cafe Stein, Vienna 1985
	Covers for listings magazine *Falter*, Vienna 1986
	Stein's Diner, Vienna 1987
	Wronkh bar/restaurant, Vienna 1989
	Helmut Lang shops, Tokyo and Osaka, Japan 1990
	Truman's shops, Salzburg and Linz, 1991
	Stadtforum, Berlin 1991
	Ungor and Klein wine shop, Vienna 1992
	Haslinger, Keck advertising agency, Vienna 1993
	Management Book Service shop, Vienna 1993
Exhibition design	'Ars Electronica', Linz 1992; Room 10, Museum of Applied Arts, Vienna 1992; Austrian Academy of Sciences 150th Anniversary 1995–

●●●ellipsis

ellipsis specialises in publishing contemporary architecture and art and culture using a range of media, from books to the world wide web. Contact us for a copy of our pocket catalogue.

... earthier than Racine, more passionate than Stendhal, more encyclopaedic than Diderot and saucier than Escoffier.
Hermine Poitou, INIT

A: 55 Charlotte Road London EC2A 3QT
E: ...@ellipsis.co.uk
w: http://www.ellipsis.co.uk/ellipsis
T: +44 171 739 3157
F: +44 171 739 3175

●●●electric editions

The ellipsis world wide web site is growing. It has been presented at numerous exhibitions and festivals, and the critics like it:

ellipsis wins. It wins with creativity. It wins with content. It wins with innovation. You need to see this site, just to get a glimpse of what online publishing can do. The overall design pulls the surfer in, with its intriguing graphical concepts, almost demands that s/he stick around for a while ... Users cruise through ellipsis pointing and clicking at icons that don't seem to make sense at first, since they rely heavily on intuitive action. But users 'learn by doing' what the different symbols and metaphors mean. It's a little complicated, but also challenging. The results are a joy to see.

This is quite possibly one of the greatest web sites I have ever visited: ever-unfolding into interactive activity, a hyperlink game, and digital transcendence. This IS the place to be.
BG, The Net magazine (USA)

The electric art cd-rom/book series was launched in March with Simon Biggs' *Book of Shadows*; number 2, *Passagen*, is due in Spring 97.

●●●paper editions

Our intention is always to publish in the most appropriate format – ranging from the interactive, intangible on-line pages of the world wide web, to the dual electronic and paper form of the electric art series, *Mekons United* with its book and audio cd, and conventional books.

These include Architecture in Context, books designed to appeal to anyone with an interest in contemporary building. The first four titles cover recent projects in Tokyo, Las Vegas, San Francisco, and Vienna. Essays provide the context necessary to understand the work – antecedents, functions, technology, urban issues – which is shown in specially commissioned photographs and drawings.

We have a paperback reprint of our very successful autobiography of Peter Rice, *An Engineer Imagines*, and a ground-breaking and very beautiful book on architecture and cyberspace, *Digital Dreams*. *The Internet and Everyone* is an important work by John Chris Jones, author of *Design Methods* and *Designing Designing*, in which he brings an unparalleled depth and range of thought to the information superhighway. Starting life on the internet, one stage of the work's development will be its existence as a book.

●●●architecture guides

The best new guides to recent architecture are published by ellipsis.
Colin Amery, The Financial Times

With a critical approach, an innovative, pocket-sized format, high-quality illustrations, and award-winning design, this series of guides – now available in English, German and French editions – describes and comments on significant contemporary architecture.

In preparation are books covering New York, San Francisco, Paris, Berlin, Sydney, Dublin, Madrid, Istanbul, Budapest, and Hong Kong, with still more to come.

Chicago: a guide to recent architecture
Susanna Sirefman
... should proved irresistible to architecture buffs.
Chicago Herald Tribune
... the perfect yuppie travel companion ... discrete enough to refer to on the Loop, potted enough to do so between stops, detailed enough to impress and indiscrete enough to entertain.
The Art Book Review Quarterly

England: a guide to recent architecture
Samantha Hardingham/photographs by Susan Benn
Latest in a delectable series ... informative, opinionated, critical text; compact, sharply printed pix. Hardingham is a positive guide to the grand, the witty, the shoddy, the soaring, the sober, the dumb.
The Observer
... remarkably up-to-date ... a fresh perspective is provided in the concise and spikily perceptive comments from the AA-trained author. The book is a pocket-sized bonus for the architecture-watcher.
Paul Finch, The Architects' Journal

London: a guide to recent architecture
Samantha Hardingham
... positively plump with exploring zeal and opinion ... Truly pocket-sized and strongly recommended.
The Observer
... it can only be applauded for broadening the audience for contemporary architecture and design.
Lorenzo Apicella, Building Design

Las Vegas: a guide to recent architecture
Frances Anderton and John Chase/photographs by Keith Collie
This is the first guide to the architecture of Las Vegas. It describes and illustrates the casinos, the hotels, and the glorious lights and neon signage of the most popular gambling mecca in the world.

Los Angeles: a guide to recent architecture
Dian Phillips-Pulverman
In the second half of this century Greater Los Angeles has become a forcing ground for avant-garde architecture, and the appetite for experiment is as strong as ever. This book describes and illustrates more than 100 buildings completed over the last ten years.

Prague: a guide to twentieth-century architecture
Ivan Margolius/photographs by Keith Collie
... up-to-date and well worth reading ... An excellent small (in size), big (in content) guide which should decorate the shelf, or rather the pocket, of any interested architect.
Robert Voticky, Building Design

Tokyo: a guide to recent architecture
Noriyuki Tajima/photographs by Keith Collie
... beautifully designed and illustrated ... Tajima's witty and enticing commentaries entice readers to make their own journeys of discovery.
Joe LaPenta, The Daily Yomiuri

Vienna: a guide to recent architecture
Ingerid Helsing Almaas/photographs by Keith Collie
... that rarity – a guide-book that is a pleasure to read in full.
The Architects' Journal

Mekons United

The Mekons were one of a group of bands to emerge from Leeds University/art school in the late 1970s. In the years since, the band has moved from punk through various musical styles, collaborated with dancers, artists and writers, and produced a stream of albums. In April 1996 an exhibition of Mekons art opened in Florida. This book presents a selection of that art, and includes a major essay by Terry Atkinson on the pop art explosion and the politics that led to punk, other essays on the economics of rock 'n' roll, the topography of Leeds, football and popular culture, art theory, and on the Mekons themselves.

The book also includes extracts from *Living in Sin*, the Mekons' novel in progress, with contributions from Kathy Acker, and a cd with more than an hour of previously unreleased Mekons music.

Mekons United is a *tour de force* from perhaps the only band that exhibits equal ability in the musical and visual arts.
Chris Morris, Billboard

Digital Dreams: architecture and cyberspace
Neil Spiller
Architecture in crisis: the era of virtual reality, cyberspace, prosthetics and nano-technology. **Secrecy and experimentation – the fears and ecstasies of the painter; the drawing as a recording of the body's creative dance.** Exploring superspace as a series of perceptual frames or surfaces with intersecting boundaries. **Surface empathy is one of the conditions of being human.** Cyberspace is another realm of architectural opportunity. **Alchemy and its transformations parallel the emergent technologies of cyberspace, nano-technology and prosthetics.** The concept of the quantum smear (the ubiquity of the electron) leads to the idea of parallel universes and the infinite states of the object.

An Engineer Imagines
Peter Rice
Now in paperback, Peter Rice's autobiography is a personal account of the joy and enthusiasm he gave to and took from his profession. Rice was widely acclaimed as the greatest structural engineer of his generation, a man who, in Renzo Piano's words, could design structures 'like a pianist who can play with his eyes shut'.

The book explains Rice's perception of, and contribution to, his most significant projects and lets the reader discover his very genuine humanity and concern for quality and sensuality. All concerned with these issues in our built environment should take the trouble to read it.
Ian Ritchie, The Architects' Journal
In *An Engineer Imagines*, the author accomplishes what was surely his principal reason for devoting his last year to this book: making vivid the process, excitement, and satisfactions of creative engineering.
Joseph Passonenneau, Architectural Record

Britain: a guide to architectural styles from 1066 to the present
Hubert Pragnell
I have a friend who once asked for a list of architectural styles to pin up in her bathroom so that she could recite them every day as she prepared for the world. She worried that she did not know when the Romanesque ended and the Gothic began. Even more worrying for some is knowing what is going on in contemporary architecture. For instance, what is post-modernism all about?

At last help is at hand ... Above all, this little book is for the beginner to take to the streets. Armed with its basics, they may find enough architectural pleasure to last a lifetime.
Colin Amery, The Financial Times

The Art of the Structural Engineer
Bill Addis
Recognition of the structural engineer's contribution to building design has grown enormously in recent years. Rather than being seen as a sobering influence on the creativity of architects, daring and innovative engineers are rightly acknowledged as creators in their own right, exploring materials and structures as part of the design team.

Engineers who read this book will come to understand architects better. It will help architects too, even if only to look at engineers in a kinder light.
Will Howie, New Civil Engineer

The Internet and Everyone
John Chris Jones
how to improve the world without making matters worse
this is the architecture of living decentrally
:prelude:
Is there something that can be added now to the idea of the internet, and to its presence, that really improves industrial life, and culture? My first answer to this question, which I wrote as an outline of this book for ellipsis and McGraw Hill, was as follows:
...

Date Wed, 25 Oct 1995 02:07:19 +0100
To ...@ellipsis.co.uk
From jcj@ellipsis.co.uk
Subject the internet & everyone

dear tom & jonathan ... & everyone
OUTLINE OF THE IDEAS
When I think of the internet I realise that, though beginning as a special medium additional to others such as surface mail, phone, fax, radio, tv, etc, it is likely to grow rapidly as a general or meta-medium (as was print and the book) that legitimises and changes the forms of all the others.

What I will be writing is my long-held view that, as computation expands, all of the specialised departments of modern life, everything from government and education to medicine and show business, will have to undergo gradual but total change or transformation as the computernet and its possibilities, threatening and benign, provoke organisations and ordinary people to develop in extraordinary ways, many of them contradictory.

That is, I will suggest that there will evolve computernet-based versions of everything, very different from the present ones (which are based on the direct presence of people in specialised roles).

The central point of this view of things is that specialisation is no longer the right form for living in industrial culture. I believe that the logic of the change from mechanical to post-mechanical, via electronic media and computing, implies that people cease to organise themselves in specialised roles, as experts highly skilled in narrowband jobs. With the aid of a computerised internet, everyone should be able to take back (from what remains of the specialised professions) the creativeness and initiative that was long ago lost to them. As I see it, the presence of accessible computing power, embedded in everything, will turn the technical know-how of experts into accessible software and their manual skills and intuitions into the normal abilities of everyone else.

The obvious precedent for this is in the early days of writing and printing. Where once there were expert scribes and readers, able to write and to print what most people could only speak, there is now widespread literacy and the recent coming of self-publishing, by computer desk-top.

Equally relevant to this is the way in which the highly complex skills of speaking and listening to colloquial speech, still beyond the abilities of computers, are not beyond the immense abilities of every single person, the gifts we were all born with. And also the way in which languages grow and change spontaneously, in ways which baffle the so-called experts in language, but without any trace of central control or design or rule by specialists.

I believe that in the immediate future of the internet the question of whether it is to grow decentrally as it began, or under the central control which the media people and the corporations would like it to become, is a main question of the time. To me, nothing else matters as much, though I suppose that is crankiness, or fanaticism. (We have to go beyond that if the future is not to be a mess!)

My purpose in writing the book is to show in some detail exactly how it is that the old path (of expert centralism) is no longer right and that the new path (of what has been called creative democracy made possible by computernet) is the right way to go. Just because it's more human, in a way that primitive industrialism never was.

In this vision of universal change from centralism to its reverse, one or two things are essential: for example, how to let go and how to keep the centre empty.

But I've not got time at the moment to say any more than that.